I have so much respec[.]
Wellbeing, she appro
dose of compassion.

Renewable Wellbeing offers a refreshing and much-needed perspective on cultivating sustainable wellbeing, both individually and collectively. Rooted in Scripture and real-life stories, Ruth Rice gently guides readers to reconsider and rejuvenate tired narratives around identity, success, community, simplicity, and vulnerability. This book is an invitation to rediscover the renewable sources of hope, joy, and purpose that are found in Christ alone. I recommend it for anyone longing for an authentic faith that translates into daily life.

Rev. Professor John Swinton. FBA, FRSE, FISSR, RMN, RNMD

I have very rarely read a book which so reflects the warmth, insight, pastoral heart and wit of the author. Ruth has wrestled with God, brokenness and wellbeing and come away with a manifesto of wisdom. With a clear take on reality she is a critical friend of the church and offers a way to start again in a sustainable, missional and hopeful way. By placing our Christian journey in (well)being, rooted in God's love our doing is authentic and renewable. It is also attractive and magnetic. If you read this book with an open and attentive heart it will transform your life.

Revd Dr Shaun Lambert, Writer, Psychotherapist,
Honorary Mindfulness Chaplain Scargill Movement

Those of us who are fans of Ruth – and I am one – will hear her voice throughout this book. The infectious, humorous, and honest person we've heard from talks and conversations comes through loud and clear.

Those of us who are supporters of Renew Wellbeing – a growing number as the number of centres continues to grow – will recognise and love the stories, gospel insights and blessings in each chapter. Most importantly, those looking for realistic sustainable help and hope for their churches will find a number of suggested changes which actually make a difference.

Ruth is a critical friend of the local church at a time when the church needs exactly this. The local church needs honest friends who are loving and supportive enough to affirm what's good alongside naming what could be better.

A loving critique for the church is easier to hear from Ruth because she brings the same level of honesty when it comes to describing the things she has gone through and is going through in her own life.

This book takes the lessons of Renew Wellbeing a step further than Ruth's previous books – providing practical help, applications and implications for the whole church.

Rev Ken Benjamin, Director of Church Relationships, LICC

An accessible well of life-giving wisdom and wellbeing. If every minister and church would draw from the waters of the simple yet profound insights in this book, lives would be helped and healed, communities would discover wellbeing not as a programme or initiative but a way of life. The book is practical, challenging, and encouraging. Drawing inspiration from John's Gospel and lived experiences, Ruth provides the reader with pathways of renewable living that would help every church to be at the heart of its neighbourhood, reflecting the gentleness of Christ and serving a flourishing of human life for all.

Roy Searle, Northumbria Community, The Commons Network, Northumbrian Collective, Pioneer Ambassador and former President, Baptist Union of Great Britain

Ruth's voice as she writes is similar to when she speaks - funny, honest, direct and prophetically insightful. But whereas a preaching voice inevitably needs volume and rhetoric to engage an audience (which Ruth is also great at) I was intrigued by the gentle tone in this book that wooed and disarmed me, and made me realise I wasn't the only one thinking and feeling and being convicted in these ways; Ruth puts words to the yearnings, hopes, and prayers for the shalom of the Kingdom of Jesus.

Martin J Young, author, leader, speaker, church planter

Come to the well and drink! Drawing profoundly on her own experience of burnout, Ruth invites us to enter God's shalom, not just for our own wellbeing but for the renewal of the church.

Whatever you believe. However you are. *Renewable Wellbeing* is for you. Discover what it is to abide in God's love.

A prophetic book that roots wellbeing not in a journey into self, but outwards into love, community and Jesus.

A must read for all, especially those involved in ministry, who are caught on the treadmill of 'doing' and 'success'. A life-giving reminder that 'it is OK not to be OK'.

Richard Atkinson, Bishop of Bedford

Renewable Wellbeing

Five culture shifts for the church

Ruth Rice

Authentic

First published 2024 by Authentic Media Limited,
PO Box 6326, Bletchley, Milton Keynes, MK1 9GG.
authenticmedia.co.uk

British Library Cataloguing in Publication Data
A catalogue record for this book is available from the British Library.
ISBN: 978-1-78893-356-8
978-1-78893-357-5 (e-book)

Cover design by Vivian Hansen (Two Rivers Creative)

Contents

.

Acknowledgements

To my lovely family and amazing team: thank you
for being you.
I'm so grateful to you and for you.
To the growing Renew Wellbeing family: there
would be no book without you.
Thank you. Sorry I couldn't include all your voices
in these pages.
And mostly thank you to the Source of all
wellbeing, who is renewing our wellbeing daily.

He himself is our peace . . .

Eph. 2:14

Introduction: What is Renewable Wellbeing?

Another wellbeing book?

This is a book about wellbeing.

. . . another book about wellbeing!

I know that wellbeing could be just another buzz word in the church as it is in many other organizations, but I believe it is the very heart of the gospel and could be the very heartbeat of our communities. I think a culture shift towards a Jesus way of wellbeing is the best hope for a tired church in a broken world.

And I think I might be seeing some evidence of just that unfolding around me: a quiet revolution of simplicity; some might even say a revival of communities of *shalom*.

The Hebrew word *shalom* has become my fascination, and since opening the doors of a simple wellbeing café run by the local church in September 2015 in Nottingham, UK, involvement in wellbeing has also been my job. I have already written about how that all came about,[1] and about what I think wellbeing might be and look like.[2]

So, what is going on with this book? Surely all the bases are covered.

The thing with wellbeing is that it is a deep well, and the more you begin to look into it as a concept and live in it as a lifestyle, the deeper it seems to be.

Being the CEO of a charity[3] with more than 250 wellbeing centres around the UK at the time of writing, my fascination with mental and emotional health, and the part the church can play in attending to community wellbeing, is growing all the time. I am always learning. Wellbeing is being lived out in simple, safe, sustainable spaces all over the UK and beyond. I am humbled to see what God is doing.

But I am also concerned.
With all the good news around the Renew movement, why am I worried?
I am concerned that this growth is a drop in the ocean.

I am concerned that there are many, many isolated folks in our communities who have no idea of the welcome of the gospel.

I am concerned that church leaders and members are burning themselves out with busyness when there is a genuine heart cry for more sustainable and authentic ways of living.

I am concerned that many of our Renew spaces are secondary to the business of running church, and that prayer is not every church's priority and heartbeat.

I am concerned that those who need the community of church the most are finding it hard to access the programmes we are so busy producing.

I don't want to start a book about the beauty of the gospel and Jesus' way of wellbeing with a negative picture of church, really I don't. I am, and always have been, a big fan of the weird little local communities of worshippers and broken folk that constitute the church. These groups of ordinary believers and seekers from all ages and backgrounds, united in their focus on God should be the safest, most welcoming places on earth for all, at any stage of their mental health journey. That is not always the case, but I sincerely believe that it could be.

In 2019 The National Churches Trust reported that there were more than 50,000 Christian congregations in the UK; that is more churches than pubs by quite a long way.[4] Each of these churches could be at the very centre of a wellbeing revolution if we would all be prepared to take a look at the Jesus way of wellbeing and be honest about a few issues that may affect the way we operate as the body of the one we believe in.

This book has been born out of this concern that is growing in me as the charity grows. Has wellbeing become the next trendy, shiny word to hook a few activities onto? Are over-busy churches simply adding in another programme to their very full schedules and tagging it as wellbeing? Or could it be that God is calling the church back into its primary language and its main calling, to practise the presence of God[5] and to be the people of prayer in ways that everyone is welcome to join in? Could wellbeing become the simple heartbeat of every church in every community?

That was my dream when we set out on this adventure.

This book comes from a heart to draw us back to the simple beauty of wellbeing as we see it in Christ. *This is a call for culture shift, not crisis management.*

This book is less about setting up wellbeing spaces and more about the big principles behind a simple way of life. *This is about wellbeing the Jesus way.*

I have always said that as a charity we don't do theological resources. Many of our friends in other charities are doing that so well. I have felt I would need a bigger brain and to be better read to theologize. But I do believe this book may well be practical theology. Theology, after all is about our thinking about God. So here are some words as I think about God as we see him in Jesus, and what he teaches us about wellbeing. Maybe it is theology. It is certainly a set of reflections from my own journey to follow Jesus into a sustainable lifestyle of *shalom* and some thoughts about how we could do that better together in churches and communities. Maybe it is an invitation for us all to become theologians.

I employ the language of food and picnics because it is practical theology.

I introduce the concept of renewable wellbeing because that is what I believe we are seeing in this movement and could see in every community.

This is a book about Jesus really. The Bible describes him as 'our peace' (Eph. 2:14).

He is wellbeing.

He is *shalom*.

We can know what God looks like because of Jesus. We can know God because of the work of Jesus on the cross. We can become like Jesus because of his resurrection and gift of the Holy Spirit in us.

The whole of the gospel is a gospel of wellbeing. Being human and honest while dwelling in a bigger story of un-changing wellbeing is what Christianity is all about. This is the very gospel needed in a broken world. It is the very gospel that accepts us and gives us life regardless of our circumstances or the state of our mental health. It is the very gospel that cries out, 'It is OK not to be OK.'[6]

But I am not convinced it is the gospel that our commu-nities are seeing us live out and I am not entirely sure that those who live around us as churches would know how to join in with our life of wellbeing in Christ or even know that the invitation is open to all.

Just looking at these Jesus stories together will help us, I hope, to believe that the language of wellbeing, which is already out there in society, is a good one for the church, as it may draw us back to the One who is the very definition of wellbeing.

This book outlines five ways of wellbeing that we see in Jesus and brings these ways alongside five big issues in the church as I see them.

Do we really need a culture shift?
The title of this book has changed as I have written it. It started out being called PICNIC, which not only drew on the picture God gave me at the start of this adventure of picnics on a battlefield, but also pointed to an acrostic that was a challenge to the church. Let me explain.

Those who have read my book *Slow Down, Show Up & Pray* will remember the importance of picnics in my own journey as a director of the mental health charity Renew Wellbeing.[7] This book is a sequel to that one, really. In that first book I tell of the vision I had of a battlefield of depression and despair and how we were invited to see that battlefield turn into a picnic site. In this vision I saw people involved in the battle lay down their arms, get up off the ground, emerge from hiding places and set up a picnic rug with a basket placed in the middle that was filled with good things to eat from above. This picture grew and developed as picnic rug after picnic rug in the places of greatest fear and struggle became places of welcome and goodness. The battlefield was becoming a picnic site.

This vision came to me at a time of recovery from my own mental and emotional breakdown. I was feeling isolated and fearful of social settings. I had begun to experience some degree of peace and wellbeing on my own at home as I engaged in hobbies and rhythms of prayer, but I still felt safest on my own at home.

I longed for a place where it was OK not to be OK. A place where I could learn to look after my wellbeing but without the social pressure to be fixed. I became fascinated with the concept of wellbeing; it is hard to define, but I came to see it as the best translation of the Hebrew word *shalom*.[8] My own journey to grasp the depth of this word 'wellbeing' led to me writing the *A–Z of Wellbeing*. I couldn't find one definition I liked but I did come up with twenty-six practices that wellbeing could look like in our lives.

It was my own struggle with low mood and anxiety that led to me set up a wellbeing space in Nottingham along with the church I was leading at the time. This space, called renew37,[9] functions like a shared front room for all. Anyone is welcome to bring a hobby or share a hobby that has helped with their wellbeing. All attending are equal; there is no 'them and us'. This is a space for all to be human together and attend to their wellbeing. Although run and funded by the local church, there is no proselyting. We are all on a journey learning to live well within our own skin when it comes to mental and emotional health, so this space became a haven for many.

Attached to the social space is a prayer space that all can access to sit quietly and reflect at any time, and where led prayers around simple patterns and rhythms take place at intervals across the session for anyone to attend should they wish to. The local church, New Life Baptist Church, Nottingham, in this case, is encouraged to partner with local mental health services and any other charities and agencies that are engaged in wellbeing.

This simple, sustainable and safe way of showing up for each other across church and community was originally intended for myself and a few others I had met who needed such a space. But lots of people began to come to the picnic rug that was renew37.

We grew to realize how vital this sort of space was for many of our regulars. Other churches started asking for help to set up similar spaces and Renew Wellbeing[10] the charity was born. This one space is now many spaces across the UK and beyond.

That story is already in print and in practice. This is not a repetition of that story, but it will draw on the lessons we are learning across the hundreds of spaces now open. The original story was mostly in my voice, as my story. This book will introduce you to many other voices across every denomination and every part of the UK.

The battlefield is becoming a picnic site.

So, you see, I love a picnic! I know they are not everyone's first choice for a meal, but to be quite honest, I can't think why not! What's not to love? You simply grab a basket, pop in what you have handy, find a place to sit, invite anyone to join you, hope they have brought some goodies too and you tuck in.
I love the simplicity.
I love the lack of preparation.
I love the inclusivity.

Picnics speak to me of meals that enable all to eat, meals that are simple and shared, meals that are held in locations where all can take part. So, this book engages the image of picnics as a vehicle to look at what wellbeing lessons we can learn from the way we share a meal – the ways Jesus shared a meal. It is about taking the habits of wellbeing out of the box, to share with all. So, calling the book PICNIC made sense to me, but anyone picking it up wanting new recipes for an outing would have been disappointed. However, the real reason for the change is deeper than that.

I was going for the title PICNIC as a dig at the church really. If you are a techie – that is, someone who loves or works in information technology – you might know PICNIC as an acrostic that stands for something a bit different.

My lovely husband, Mark, works in IT for a city council and as we both work from home he also does a lot of pro bono work for Renew Wellbeing! My plaintive cry that the 'stupid laptop has broken again', or that there is 'something wrong with this programme' is often met with the response: 'I think you will find that's a PICNIC problem.'

Having thought I had stumbled on an issue that could help millions, I discovered this expression was not at all flattering. A PICNIC problem stands for:

Problem
In
Chair
Not
In
Computer

In other words: I am the problem, not the machine I am using. Fair comment, actually.

As I considered the growing need for shared wellbeing habits in our communities and churches, and pondered the issues that have concerned me enough to make me want to write this book, I sensed that the letters of the word 'picnic' could lead us to acknowledge our own Christian version of the acrostic:

Problem
In
Church
Not
In
Christ

It is my belief that people in general are hungry for the love of God and the freedom that Jesus brings, for the life of the Spirit of God that is *shalom*. Real wellbeing. Real peace.

I was convinced that the problem lay with the church. Without wanting to offend all those who have poured their lives into church structures for many years (I am one of them), I believe we are being invited into simpler, safer and more sustainable ways of being church in a world in need of communities of wellbeing. But I cannot put my name to a book that is critical of the church. I can't because that is not God's heart. He loves his bride . . . fiercely.

In fact, as I wrote the book and listened to the stories coming out of the 270-plus Renew centres nationwide, my heart was warmed and encouraged by the amazing wellbeing spaces and the people finding peace and hope in many, many places. Some churches are letting the Renew principles leak into the rest of their church life, with prayer undergirding everything and partnership enabling God's people to make a simple offer of presence that is sustainable. Some churches are changing their Sunday gatherings to make them more accessible to those who are anxious.
So, I am heartened.

The concern is still there, though. Not enough for me to keep a title that levelled blame at God's beautiful broken church that he loves, but enough to make me want to articulate the five areas I think need to be addressed if we are to see a change of culture that enables the church to thrive and wellbeing to be renewed. The culture shift should point our gaze to Jesus' love, not the church's faults.

I have been challenged by the story of Gideon in the book of Judges recently. In this story, Gideon is chosen to fight a battle he felt ill prepared for, with an army that God pruned right back to very, very few. As I looked out over the vast and growing need in the mental and emotional health of our nations, the battle felt huge and the idea of picnics on a battlefield, quite frankly, felt ridiculous, small, silly.

Gideon is led to take a secret wander round the enemy camp and listen. He hears people talking of dreams they have had of being beaten and he takes courage from what he hears. Having been emptied of all his own power, he relies solely on God's power and with a trumpet sound and clay jars broken to reveal the light the enemy is defeated.

Our battle is not against people, it is against a growing despair that grips people's hearts and minds. The news beamed into our living rooms doesn't help. The world feels much shakier than ever. I am hearing of more suicides through our networks than ever before. Church leaders are weary and volunteer workforces are depleted. We are not OK.

But as I am wandering around the battlefield of despair and isolation, I am finding that God is out there and many in our churches are dreaming dreams of a new way of being. Renew Wellbeing's message has a place to land and it is landing. Someone told me this week that they loved the new way of being church and doing life that Renew had taught them. My heart leapt. A new way of being church and doing life! Not a new thing to do to help the poor, ill people, no . . . a new way of doing life!

Yes! This is the culture shift I long to see. A gentler, more Christlike way of living, worshipping, belonging and sharing good news. I believe people will come flocking to find Jesus when the church really engages in the habits of life that he shows us and wins for us at the cross. True *shalom* as a lifestyle could spark a quiet revival.

To enable all to access the beauty of the ways of wellbeing of Jesus, I believe we are being called to a deeper consideration of what wellbeing looks like in his life and ministry.

We are being invited to a table spread with goodness open to all. We are being welcomed to tap into a source of wellbeing that will *never* run out! In short, it's time to do away with some of the old sources of power and wellbeing we have been relying on and to connect in all our ways to the source of *shalom* that is renewable.

What is renewable wellbeing?
So why change to *Renewable Wellbeing* as a title, you might ask?

I think many of us are concerned about the wellbeing of our beautiful planet and the need to reduce emissions and find more sustainable ways of consuming and producing energy.

Now, I am no scientist and I am coming very late to the conversation about renewables, but as I borrow the word 'renewable' to apply to our whole lives, I want to make sure I honour the work that has gone in to drawing our attention to this vital concept, and I want to continue to personally make sure I try to live more carefully in my own use of resources. This is not a scientific book. I think you will have spotted that. This is an honest reflection on wellbeing and, as such, this concept of renewable sources of energy brings me to an important realization:

> We need to find ways of living with renewable energy, renewable hope, renewable love, renewable life if we are to be flourishing communities of wellbeing.

My own story of burnout, of using up all my energy, all my hope, all my *shalom* and finding myself beyond empty has not only led me to the habits and practices that now form a way of life and leading, but that season led me to see many, many others who were also crying out with exhaustion, isolation and mental ill health. I met so many people in the shadows of community hiding like I was. I heard the thin cry of despair like I had never heard it before, and I was undone by it.

Renewability in power sources is a key factor in caring for our hurting planet. We will need to let go of some of the old ways of powering our lives and take a few risks if we are to meet our renewable energy targets.

In our wellbeing, our *shalom*, our sense of peace and wholeness as individuals and communities, we need to tap into a source of *shalom* that will not run out. I think the local church holds the keys to what that source could look like in practice.

The old ways of sourcing wellbeing and energy in the church through many meetings, invitational effort and busy rotas may need to give way to engage with more sustainable ways. I would love to see more simple habits, lifestyle changes, deeply prayerful practices that gently shift our culture towards knowing our identity, measuring success differently, being community radically, having simplicity of habits that we share daily and grasping the truth that failure is an option as we engage in renewability.

This phrase 'renewable wellbeing' is something that I believe is a description of all the life I am witnessing in the Renew Wellbeing spaces so far. It encompasses not just a feeling of wellbeing that can be attained, but a state of wellbeing that we can dwell in by realizing it is renewable – it can be made new in us and through us. Here and now.

But to engage in this renewable wellbeing, and not just have more wellbeing programmes, there are five key culture shifts that I think need our attention:

1. Identity: There is a crisis of identity going on in society and also maybe in the church around our grasp of God's real identity and ours.
2. Economy: The measures being used for what constitutes success are flawed and have leaked into the church. The way of the cross and the economy of 'the one' is vital.
3. Community: The church is part of its community and needs to sit without power to learn the ways of wellbeing together. Wellbeing can never be just a personal thing.
4. Simplicity: There needs to be a radical return to the simple ways of the Christian life that are shareable.
5. Vulnerability: It is essential to embrace our brokenness and hear God's call within our vulnerability if we are to be able to give anything at all and lead from our lives.

Who is the book for?

I believe it is the local church together that can sustain the presence, prayerfulness and partnership that is needed to see wellbeing shared and restored in our communities. This book is aimed at churches and church leaders. But my prayer is it will have something in it for anyone with a pulse.

You see, when I set up the first Renew space it was as a broken leader with a dear church behind me, not simply an individual wanting to recover. I saw this Renew idea as a way of leading with wellbeing, not just living with wellbeing, and it was sad to keep hearing in meetings: 'What shall we do about clergy mental health?'

It has been heart-breaking to hear about worn out and suicidal leaders when I believe there is a gentler way to live and lead. Church could be part of the answer to the wellbeing crisis, not part of the problem, as it is for some who lead.

If you lead or are part of a church, I pray that this book will help you towards a gentler DNA for a more sustainable lifestyle. If you are on a journey of faith and have not found a community to call home, then I pray that this book might help you find what you are looking for and deepen your own wellbeing foundations.

As we begin to see new ways of being gathered church forming alongside these Renew spaces, I have put together some ideas for how to use each chapter not only for personal study and reflection but also as a basis for shared life too.

At the end of each chapter there will be ideas for how to:

a. Be present: these are ways you can engage personally with the story and can be used on your own.

b. Be prayerful: these are suggestions for going even deeper into the story in communication with God either on your own or with others on retreat.
c. Be in partnership: these ideas and questions could form the basis of a group or gathering.

Within each chapter you will hear the voices of members of the Renew family around the UK. These are people who are living these principles and the stories; examples and quotes might help all of us realize this is a way of life to be lived, not a theory to be read about and put on a shelf.

The book is shaped around the Five Ways to Wellbeing.[11] These five things that help our *shalom* came from some research a number of years ago, but I believe they still give us a language and a way of being that connect us with a hunger and need that is already out there. The five ways are:

Connecting
Learning
Getting active
Taking notice
Giving

These five things are meant to structure activity when used therapeutically. But I have used them in my own life and across the charity to also help us talk about what is going on in our inner lives, our 'off-stage' lives.

Churches have been engaging in these ways to wellbeing for centuries, connecting with God and one another, learning how to follow him, read his Word and do what he says. We are getting active in his world as we serve others, but also in our inner habits as we spend time getting to know God more. We are taking notice in the disciplines of stillness, silence and worship. We are giving ourselves outwardly, our time and our resources, but also inwardly submitting to God's call and ways.

I will employ these five ways as I examine five episodes in the life and teaching of Jesus in the Gospel of John that challenge us about connecting around the issue of identity, learning the new economy of the kingdom, getting active in community with what we have, not what we don't have, taking notice of simplicity and the lack of it in our habits and finally giving in renewable ways, sensing our call to serve that comes from brokenness and forgiveness.

These are five episodes from the life of Jesus as, whether you follow him or not, I believe him to be the very best example of what it looks like to live with wellbeing in human skin. These stories teach us loads of things, but I will be drawing out from them the points that have struck me on my wellbeing journey. This is a sort of simple theology that is still developing and an invitation for you to address some of the wellbeing issues in your life, leadership and church as you walk through these stories with me. These stories are all picnics of a sort, so the original title lives on! There is food and drink involved anyway, and a sense of sharing what is on offer even if there is no basket or rug. This will always be about those picnics on the battlefield.

Come with me as we walk the wellbeing way with the One who made us, knows us and still loves us completely. Come and be renewed from the source of all wellbeing.

Here are some thoughts as we begin from one of our Renew hosts and Local Links in London.

From awkward inaction to prayerful presence: Renew in London

For many years I had felt concerned that the church wasn't really addressing mental health issues. As a practice nurse, I felt frustrated that we had little time to support patients with their mental health struggles, and yet it was so evident that their physical problems were compounded by their mental ones. So as I approached retirement I prayed about what God would have me do next. When I heard about Renew Wellbeing I was really interested in the idea. Once I had read Ruth's book, I knew that I should explore the possibility of starting a Renew group in our church, and thankfully the pastor and elders were in agreement. I was able to identify two 'people of peace'[12] from our congregation almost immediately. They 'got it' and were keen to come on board. Over time, three others have joined our team. Every host has their own personal testimony of mental health challenges, either their own, or those of someone close to them. Every one of them brings their own unique gifts to the table. I love this. As a group we have become very close, and seek to support each other as much as we can. Although we are not a 'house group' or a 'life group', in some ways we fulfil the role of one, and we share our burdens and pray for one another. One of our team worships at a different church, which further enriches our fellowship.

However, we are all mindful of the need to be completely inclusive during our Renew sessions. We endeavour to mingle among the guests and avoid an 'us/them' mentality. It was originally thought that Renew might not adapt well to large cities like London, but we think it does! Wherever they live, people experience the same needs for identity and community, and in some ways even more so where the pace of life and the transient nature of the population is greater. Loneliness is a very real problem for many of our guests. We have found that although the activities on offer are welcomed by some, many more enjoy the human connection, and the chance just to 'be' around others. We have seen people who were initially very shy and anxious return with a completely different demeanour, looking relaxed and chatting freely with others guests.

In the wake of Covid, many similar groups have been set up in and around Ealing. What makes Renew different? Prayer. Prayer is the bedrock on which Renew is founded and thrives. I have been so encouraged to see people with no previous experience of prayer eagerly participate in, and really appreciate, our prayer times . . . and, of course, we as hosts pray, not just for each other but for our guests. We see our prayers answered and we see God at work. He is so good.[13]

Frances Dalton, July 2023

Identity: Connecting with God and Ourselves

Connecting with the bigger story

One of the biggest issues in our society is that of identity. The phrase 'identity crisis' was introduced by psychologist Erik Erikson (1902–94) in the middle of the twentieth century.[1] I am no expert, but the phrase echoes within me as something we really need to address if we are serious about exploring wellbeing both personally and as a society. Big questions about who we are, what our story is and who we think God is are foundational to what we will believe about wellbeing. I think there is an identity crisis in many of our churches about who we are as the body of Christ and what the gospel really is.

> THOUGHT: Identity is really key: who you think you are and who you think God is will affect your wellbeing.
> QUESTION: Who am I? Who is he? Who are we?

Connecting with my story: My identity

To lead or follow with any degree of wellbeing, I think we need to be able to tell our own stories, to reflect on our own path and to continually find ourselves in God's bigger story. Here are some of my reflections on my own story to ground the principles of *shalom* that I will explore in my everyday life. I pray that you too will be able to find voice for your stories and value your own reflections.

My journey to becoming a person fascinated with wellbeing and God began early in life when my identity was being formed.

Many of my earliest memories are church ones. We spent a lot of time in church! I have written at length about my mental health experience in previous books[2] and this won't be a repeat of that part of the story. It involved a mental health crisis which was effectively a long season of burnout that led to me setting up the Renew Wellbeing charity. But when I look back at the roots of my obsession with wellbeing and my struggles with my own identity I find it, surprisingly, in my lovely, trauma-free, idyllic seaside childhood.

My family are the best of people. I was never in any doubt of how loved I was. I know that people who have had a really hard time and continue to do so must be yelling at these pages right now. What on earth was I doing having a mental health crisis when I had such a fantastic start in life, such a delightful place to live? To add insult to injury, for those wondering about my very ordinary story, I went on to have a job I loved in teaching, a loving husband, a great family . . . seriously, why couldn't I just be grateful and get on with it? I have yelled those facts and questions at myself often enough, believe me!

Yet somehow, somewhere down the line, with all that love and beauty around me, I managed to develop a sense of my own and God's identity that drove me, rather than led me, to the very brink of my own sanity. Much of what I decided about myself and how God must feel about me, and by extension what I needed to do and be to be acceptable to everyone, was fabricated in my own overactive head. For me there is no blame exercise in this exploration of identity. That is not the case for everyone and my prayer is that you find helpful, honest ways to take a good long look at what formed your ideas of identity as you read these words.

I wonder what it is about the human mind that causes it to focus in on the negative and the critical so much when surrounded by so many other signs of love and acceptance? You know how it is. You finish a preach, or a task, and several people thank you or say something encouraging, but there is one sour face, one throwaway remark about how long you went on, or even one person who usually says something and their silence is loud for you.

Which of these people's responses will you fixate on all day? Well, if you are anything like me (and I know not all of you are!), it will be the negative or perceived negative comment. I think I am a serial people pleaser in recovery.

So, with all the positives in my early life, all the goodness and beauty, all the seaside trips and tram rides, all the great times at a safe and loving church, how is it that I picked up the impression of a God who was generally a bit disappointed with me and loved me despite my character, not because of it? How did I decide to follow a God who was committed to changing me into someone much better at being a Christian and who would be really hard to please, when my role models had never ever given me the impression that love had to be earned? In fact, growing up, my sisters and I were fairly lazy, to be honest, as our lovely parents over-praised us for doing very little. The bar was low. We were and are loved unconditionally, which is a rare gift, I know.

But even with all this, my earliest memories at church and Sunday school, the stories I really engaged with, were the ones where we narrowly avoid God's judgement, where the good people just about get away with it and get God's favour.

I loved the stories of Noah and Jonah. I felt I might be called to build an ark, or even if I ran away from a great calling I would be delivered back to my 'world-changing destiny' by a large fish or some other miraculous transport method. I wanted to be Daniel and be the best prayer warrior in the land and to stand firm in the face of lions. I felt an affinity with David, and loved the telling and retelling in many and varied church events of the giant-killing capacity of a young man. In short, I was raised on amazing stories of valiant people of God, and

I wanted to be one! You will notice if you are a Bible scholar that most of the stories that I loved were Old Testament, pre-Jesus coming.

There were plenty of Jesus stories too and I loved them, but they seemed a little too gentle and lacking in *umph* for me. I did genuinely feel grateful for the cross and loved the person of Jesus as I understood him, even as a little girl, but I think I really believed I needed Jesus so that I could be a more valiant version of my Old Testament heroes.

For those reading this who have not had a one-track Christian upbringing, I apologize. I imagine you also had stories and impressions of goodness and heroic behaviour that formed you. It was maybe just a little less 'in your face' than my church-focused upbringing.

I want to bring you to a story I almost never heard as a flannel-board presentation or puppet show in all my Sunday school moments. I want to explore the depths of this story with you because I am beginning to realize that I never met this God in my younger days. I think if had I met this person, this identity of my Maker, I might have had a slightly different view of my own life and of the lives of others.

I am beginning to understand, in my own life, that identity is a key issue. Knowing who I am and knowing what God is like, is at the very heart of my wellbeing adventure.

As mentioned earlier, I am using the Five Ways to Wellbeing as a framework for this book, as it is a language already out there as people in general search for meaning and peace. The first way is to connect. For me, this is connecting with God first, then with myself and thus with others and the world around me. How I connect with the big story, the character of God, affects how I feel about everything else.

We connect with our own wellbeing stories in our daily habits and practices. But it is really important that the One we are connecting with in these habits isn't actually a false image of God. In this book I will be exploring how the connection with God in the person of Jesus can help us with wellbeing. If, for you, your wellbeing story is based on a different world view, then please use these steps to help you explore that. But if, like me, you have based your entire life and being on connecting with the God who made and loves you, I would invite you to dig a bit deeper into what you really believe about the character of this God with whom you seek to connect each day in wellbeing habits.

If this God is disappointed and generally sighing at your choices and behaviour (or at least, that's how you have come to view him), if this God is expecting so much from you that the best you can do is run to try to keep up with his expectations, and your usual choice is to keep your head down and feel like you could do better, be better, if this God is not all love, all kindness, then you may have decided to stop connecting altogether.

So here is a story that I keep coming back to, as I feel like I might have missed something, not having heard this one much earlier on when I formed my views about God.

Connecting with his story: His identity
One of my habits since my recovery is to read a bit of a gospel each day alongside my psalm and whatever else I am reading or studying in the Bible. This constancy of learning Jesus, looking at Jesus, is helping me to renew a distorted image of God through my own fascination with what God looks like in the person of Christ. To start each day dwelling in a Jesus story helps me look at what God looks like through the lens of what he showed us when he came and took on human skin. If we are to live with wellbeing in our own lives, I would suggest that the person of Jesus provides us with the very best example ever seen in history of how to understand wellbeing.

This is only one story of Jesus among many, but I believe every recorded story is there for a reason and points us to the whole character of God and the whole message of the gospel. Every word of the gospels leads us to the death and resurrection of God himself in human form and the ushering in of a new kingdom, a new covenant and a new way of understanding *shalom* or wellbeing.

Having been so fascinated with becoming an Old Testament hero when I was a child, I now find myself daily being thankful that I live this side of the cross, which brings me into a whole new understanding of God's love and mercy and my own identity.

So here we have it. A deep dive into a gospel story.

All of the stories in this book are taken from the Gospel of John, as I mentioned above, which has become a firm favourite – I feel like I'm reading the words of someone who knew and loved Jesus well. The old me would have liked a gospel written by Peter, hot-headed and a bit self-obsessed, or even someone who didn't get to follow Jesus closely but watched from a jealous distance. I think I really concocted a gospel through the eyes of St Paul in my own hot-headed student days, when I knew all the answers but none of the right questions. Mine was a judgemental, 'try harder' view of God, not just for me but for everyone else. In my gentler, emotionally unhealthy, limping years I fell in love with John's gospel and have been fascinated with it ever since.

Come with me as I follow Jesus into this simple, ordinary, everyday miracle. It was the one I rarely heard in Sunday school. I wonder if it felt a bit too frivolous a miracle to instil in us a healthy fear of God? I wonder even if a miracle where Jesus seems to condone excessive alcohol consumption might have felt a little counter-productive for my teetotal teachers?

The wedding at Cana
Take some time to read this familiar story again.

> On the third day there was a wedding at Cana in Galilee, and the mother of Jesus was there. Jesus also was invited to the wedding with his disciples. When the wine

ran out, the mother of Jesus said to him, 'They have no wine.' And Jesus said to her, 'Woman, what does this have to do with me? My hour has not yet come.' His mother said to the servants, 'Do whatever he tells you.'

Now there were six stone water jars there for the Jewish rites of purification, each holding twenty or thirty gallons. Jesus said to the servants, 'Fill the jars with water.' And they filled them up to the brim. And he said to them, 'Now draw some out and take it to the master of the feast.' So they took it. When the master of the feast tasted the water now become wine, and did not know where it came from (though the servants who had drawn the water knew), the master of the feast called the bridegroom and said to him, 'Everyone serves the good wine first, and when people have drunk freely, then the poor wine. But you have kept the good wine until now.' This, the first of his signs, Jesus did at Cana in Galilee, and manifested his glory. And his disciples believed in him.

John 2:1–11

This is the first miracle of Jesus recorded in John's gospel, and what a strange one to start with. John is most definitely taking us on a journey in his beautiful writings. This is an adventure to open up a mystery of God's love to us. And this is where he chooses to begin.

In many ways it isn't surprising there weren't many Fuzzy Felt[3] depictions of this one, or many children's storybooks with this as the big story. It feels out of keeping with the rest of the miracles. It feels a little bit like Jesus only does this one to please his mum. As a parent, I don't see any problem with that, to be honest! But this is the story I find myself occupied with in this season of my life. I find myself asking why John would think this was the best way to introduce the One who is the way, truth and life.[4]

On the surface of it, this seems a pretty unnecessary miracle. I was led to believe that everything Jesus did had purpose, and everything was for the benefit of the most needy. You can hardly call under-catering a major life disaster, can you? In the culture of the ancient Near East, however, to run out of wine would be a shameful thing and bring disrepute on the family. But it still feels like a problem they should have and could have sorted themselves.

This is a lavish family occasion that Jesus seems to have been invited to because of his mum. The disciples were there too. Maybe he was invited as the new rabbi in the making, but it is so early in his ministry it is more likely that this is simply a family wedding or neighbourhood event that all friends and family were invited to. We've all been to those. At the time of writing, we have just hosted our son and daughter-in-law's wedding in our garden. It was glorious. There was enough wine. Enough of everything, really. That was down to good planning on my children's part, and I don't think we would have expected any divine intervention if we hadn't planned well enough. We would have just popped to the shops or invited people to drink less. I know this wedding in Cana was in very different times. No popping to the shops, and wine was really the only safe thing to drink when the water wasn't that drinkable.

Even so!
Water into wine . . .
At a wedding!

Could this really be important enough to take up half a chapter of John's whole account of what it looks like to be God in human skin?

I wonder if you too sidelined this story as you began your relationship with this Jesus? Many, like me, were raised on stories of much more worthy God encounters than an encouragement to have some good wine.

What is it that draws me – as a busy Christian activist and a people pleaser in recovery – back time and again to this starting point, this simple story?

I tend to approach these Jesus stories as if I am observing them at the time. I usually look at them from the viewpoint of the disciples. You may want to place yourself somewhere else to watch what unfolds. As a follower of Jesus I, at this point, would have no real idea who I was following. Both Andrew and Philip seem to have got excited by the possibility that this was the Messiah[5] and encouraged others to follow, but up to this point only John the Baptist had done any proclaiming.[6]

So, this wedding was their first outing as Jesus' followers, and they may well have been expecting some sign or other. But they could just have been pleased to get some free food and a chance to spend time with their new leader.

When Mary approaches Jesus with the problem of the wine running out, he appears to dismiss her suggestion that he should be involved. It seems to be in response to her firm belief that he will have compassion and power to do something that he does the miracle. It is his mum's faith and insistence that seems to change an ordinary family occasion into a gospel-worthy miracle moment. Jesus appears to do something to please his mother. Could it possibly be so? Here is the first thing that is re-forming my understanding of God's identity and my own.

Jesus does care about the ordinary days and is present in the seemingly unimportant details of our lives

As I read over and over this brief exchange between mother and son that leads to the first display of God's power in the person of Jesus, I can't help but conclude that this looks very much like a mother who believed in her son, and a son who wanted to help out his mum's friends. As a parent it feels quite familiar, and I had never spotted it in the story before. My view of the character of God as seen in Jesus has always been fuelled by the wonderful, the amazing, the powerful, the extraordinary, the great, massive sacrifice, the shining resurrection glory – not by a man caring about his mother and the party he was at.

In many ways I had pushed Jesus to the edges of my own human experience and then run myself ragged trying to join him in an adventure that had little to do with my everyday life. But here is a God who comes to my family events, who cares about my bad planning, who brings the extraordinary into the ordinary and who may respond to my pleas for help, even if it wasn't his first thought and wasn't that important in the greater scheme of things.

His miraculous provision is a response to Mary's ask, in fact wasn't even an ask. She tells him there is an issue then she instructs those around her to 'Do whatever he tells you' (John 2:5). It is a shocking piece of assumption that only a mum could get away with.

In the other miracles recorded in John there is a needy person who asks for help or someone close to them who cries out on their behalf, or at least Jesus is responding to a real-life threatening situation.
There is the healing of the official's son in John 4:46–54.
There is the healing of the man by the pool in John 5:1–11.
There is the feeding of the 5,000 in John 6:1–14.
Then there is the water walking in John 6:16–21.
The healing of the man born blind in John 9:1–12.
The resurrection of Lazarus in John 11.

These, together with the water into wine miracle, are often referred to as the 'Seven Signs of John' in a New Creation theology. In this school of thought this first miracle is a sign pointing to the 'hour' when he will give his life for us. In saying to Mary that his 'hour has not yet come' (John 2:4) he opens up to us the fact that there is an 'hour', a plan, a mission, that will come. This is all true and could very well be the only purpose of this miracle. But I tend to think these stories can teach us far more than the one thing our theologians have decided they mean.

Here we have Jesus, the King of kings, the One who is 'the way' (John 14:6) taking time to make sure a family wedding goes well. He doesn't keep doing this. His ministry isn't some sort of weird wine production show. He knows what his calling is, he knows what is important. But in all of this divine knowing, it seems not to be simply about hard and fast rules. It is not a 'head down: no distractions' sort of walk he takes through his few short years on earth.

He is fully engaged in life.

He goes to a wedding.

He stays for the party.

He helps when there is a catering issue.

He is present in the ordinary day.

He inhabits human skin.

So do we.

I am beginning to see how much Jesus still wants to be invited to our ordinary events, how much he still wants to stay for the party.

Even in my illness I played a ridiculous game of trauma top trumps with God. My prayers often went something like this:

> I don't deserve your help, Lord. I should be able to cope. I am so sorry I can't pull myself out if this. I should be able to, with all you have given me. I should be more grateful. I need you, but there are so many people who need you more. I am so sorry. Please help me. But don't worry if you are too busy helping someone who really

needs it. I'm not too bad and should be OK soon and I can manage. Sorry.

Ridiculous, right? And indicative that I had not understood the character of the one I follow at all. As if he could be limited to only really 'important' things. As if he judged situations like that anyway.

This is the God who took time to make some really good wine at a wedding!

This is a God who wasted a miracle on under-catering.

Even that statement makes it sound like God is a genie and we have three wishes!

This is a fully present, living, loving, breathing Saviour.

At the wedding.

Staying for the party.

Interested in my ordinary days.

Willing to respond to the cheeky ask and daring faith of another.

Jesus takes the religious, empty things and fills them with better than the best

The other surprising thing about this story, that leads me to think I might have missed something in my desire to know the bigger story I am connecting to in wellbeing, is what Jesus does next. In response to his mum's faith, he simply looks around him and uses what is to hand, which happens to be religiously symbolic water jars. These would be ready for washing and purifying people from sin. So, to find Jesus using these very jars to make more wine would have been a shocking thing to religious folk. And we can assume this to be a religious household by the very presence of the purification jars in the first place.

Here Jesus begins his ministry by risking offending people. Religious people. He takes what had tied people to law and guilt, and fills it with something that speaks of life – water – which becomes something that speaks of celebration – wine. This may even have links to his teaching on living water, and his use of wine to depict his blood that will be shed for us. There are so many levels on which Jesus is teaching us, showing us, being with us here. But at a very basic human level, as a disciple watching on, here is just a wonderful miracle of water turned to wine, and wine is flowing out of jars that were meant to be *only* used for religious washing.

Here I am engaging on a whole new level, as I read this, with a God who renews our old religious ways. For me, that has meant a whole fresh look at what I believe about the gospel, what I believe about God himself, what I believe about wellbeing, and how that affects the way I live. I am living in this every day and hope the adventure of these mysteries takes me through all my breathing days.

I am inviting him to make better use of the old jars of using prayer as a way to worry with my eyes shut, of exhausting myself in the pursuit of pleasing God, of attending so many church meetings I had little time to be church in my own family, of judging myself and others by unreachable standards, of thinking that I could study my way into God's good books and work my way into being someone more loved.

I am seeing him filling those old ways with his water that becomes wine in the pouring, and not just any wine, either. He seems to save the best until last. He can redeem our older years with even more learning and fresh revelations.

Connecting with our story: The church's identity and the Renew Wellbeing experiment

Coming full circle, I find myself pondering what this could all have to do with us as the body of Christ, as the church, as communities? If there is a problem in church and not in Christ (and it is fine to completely disagree with me on this, of course!), what is the problem that exists with our identity as church and could be helped by the identity of God as seen in Jesus in this story?

As I see it, after spending more than half a century giving my time and energy to the organization that we call 'church' in pursuit of knowing and pleasing God, a decade of that serving as a church leader full-time and approaching a decade running a Christian charity, I still love the local church – really, I do.

I don't see another organization anywhere that welcomes anyone to join it regardless of status, ability, age, gender, ethnicity, or any other factors. This family that Jesus came to get started and connect to one another for life and love is still the best way to enact in everyday life what Jesus came to begin.

However, as a family or a body, both of which are great images for church, it is also a bit fractured, a bit broken, and full of very ordinary humans who make mistakes. This should be our biggest selling point, but the identity crisis I think the church may be having and may have been having for centuries is one of forgetting we are also human.

I have sat through many a sermon where we are reminded that we are 'not of this world' (John 18:36), that we are children of a different kingdom, that this world is not our home. I have sat through very few that remind us we are human, we are living here in real bodies, real homes, with other real people and that we will fail. I have preached the 'glory, glory, aren't we amazing' sermons myself. I have also done a fair few 'aren't we all rubbish' ones too. What I am only just digging into is the talk based on this passage of Scripture that says: Jesus wants to be in your ordinary life, he cares about the things you've got wrong or forgotten and he will stay for the party. He will take your old dusty religious practices and fill them with life.
He is present.
He was invited and he came.
He is still here.

Now, if the ordinary, the everyday, the waking and the sleeping, the family times and lonely times all matter to him, it might just affect the way we see and talk about church.

At present we tend to ask if people 'go to' church. This implies church is a place, a meeting, an event. But when

Jesus invites us to be followers, he wants us to follow him into everyday occasions as well as holy ones. It seems to me that what Jesus came to start and what we now call 'church' bear little resemblance to one another.

The identity of the One who used his first miracle to replace old stuffy religious practices with fresh, living, flowing wine seems to have got a little lost in the gathered events we treasure and work so hard to put on.

For me it took a breakdown to reimagine what church could become. I found the way we gathered on Sundays so hard to access when I was unwell. I so needed people to share the silences, to help me hold to the simple practices of prayer, meditation and hobbies that would restore my soul. There is still, of course, a place for celebration, for big gatherings, for teaching the Word, for practices that unite us, like sung meditation (or 'worship songs', as we call them). I for one would be the poorer without them. But if we are *being* church not just *going to* church, then there need to be many and varied ways of making space for God's presence and for each other.

This miracle of water into wine leads me to believe that the new wine is still being poured from the old religious jars.

What we are seeing in the Renew Wellbeing movement is just one of the ways we are witnessing God filling the jars we have and pouring them out in our communities.

In Renew spaces, we come together as humans, not experts. We come to give but we also come to receive. We come empty, rather than full of what we want to do. We come to practise the presence of God[7] in spaces open to all and we see his presence in not just the prayer times, but in the faces of those he has made. We see him in the details, the hobbies, the shared cups of tea. We see him in the silences and the desire to just show up. We see him in the very ordinary and broken moments, as well as in the loud noise and big group gathering.

The amazing thing is that many others are seeing him too. Many are finding faith for the first time or coming back to God's peaceful presence for the hundredth time. In this weird little miracle of just showing up and being human together, of praying simple prayers and sharing a space without power, it seems connection is happening.

Many of us are connecting to God in ways that deepen our grasp of his identity simply by being around others and learning together. Many are finding themselves hungering for God in the silence of the prayer spaces. And as we connect more deeply with the God who shows up in our ordinary moments, we find ourselves connecting better with our own identity as individuals and as communities of wellbeing.

Finally, I bring us to the last great identity crisis, which I think might actually be the identity of the gospel itself. Many of us are coming to believe that this gospel might actually be better news than we thought. This might well be really good news for all, even for those who had experienced it as bad news in the past, those who have felt excluded because they couldn't sing the songs or attend the big meetings, those who struggled to accept themselves and who walked a lonely path. Some of us are connecting with each other in new ways and it smells a bit like heaven. It feels like the best wine is flowing from the old religious jars and it is surprisingly delicious. You could even say it's the best wine we have ever tasted.

The Renew Wellbeing story: Living our new identity
This is not just my experience. We have seen Renew spaces open across the country in many and varied churches, we have heard stories of new wine flowing in old, stuck religious ways.

Here are a few of the stories . . . there are many more. God is still in the wine-making business wherever he sees some dusty old religious vessels waiting around.

Fiona's story: From a big and distant entity to a side-by-side friend
I was brought up in a loving, Christian home and a strict non-conformist church setting where men were in leadership. As an opinionated, headstrong young person this could be a bit challenging at times, and eventually after a relationship breakdown in my early twenties I moved into a more relaxed church environment. Having asked Jesus into my life at 11, I was baptized at 14 and that was it, really; I knew I was supposed to have a 'relationship' with God but never really worked out what that looked

like for myself. *To me, God was a big and distant entity who had lots of rules.* I was running around, trying to do good things, joining in all the church activities, making myself indispensable (or so I thought!) when in my late thirties, I had a large stroke after a car accident which left me in a wheelchair and dependent on my parents for everything. So, in my mind, this distant God had punished me for years of neglect, and I had nothing to say to him apart from, 'Why me?' I suppose I felt that God was very big, and I was very small and not worth bothering with! Thankfully, that was never the case; I was just not seeing or hearing properly.

Almost a decade later, I was introduced to Renew Wellbeing and the lights started to go on. I was advised to go back and read the gospels; *really* read the gospels, and I met properly with the Jesus that I know and love today. John 4, where Jesus meets the Samaritan woman at the well, showed me a God who chooses to spend time with unexpected people and breaks down perceived social barriers. Could I be one of those unexpected people? In the past I could have talked endlessly about car interiors (my previous job), but wouldn't have the audacity to talk about my weekly learnings from God. Now, a bit like the woman at the well, I want to share the way Jesus choses to spend time with us (modelled in our Renew spaces) with everyone.

These days, *God and I travel along side-by-side and talk daily, it's a much healthier relationship*![8]

Fiona is a much-valued member of our Renew team and I love the journey she is on with God, and her honesty and enthusiasm. The way her view of God has changed is one of the most delightful things that the Renew rhythms and way of being can bring.

Jonathan's story: Becoming wholly who I am in my completeness

Jonathan is the Renew area coordinator for Scotland and a Baptist minister:

> I'll start with me. A Christian for forty-one years at the start of my RW[9] journey. Largely schooled in evangelical ways – so a strong ethic of witness/discipleship and 'doing'. I am also someone who has had a 'a role' in nearly all of my church life – leader, principally – someone that others look to and rarely, if ever, just one of the crowd. I have always been busy in church life – and sometimes unapproachable because of that. In one sense, that is what God has called me to but then, of *course,* it becomes hard to let go and to *not* be in charge – or, indeed, to really stay dependent on God. In the RW session which we have, I can absolutely let 'a role' go, and so it is one of those situations where I do not sense major expectations on me for the structure or process – or indeed the outcomes. I do have a role, of course, in planning, and so there is work and effort because it should fulfil its purpose well, *but* the call to keep it simple is helpful. The RW session does not carry the usual pressures that happen for most Christian activity for me.

In terms of how I have seen myself and my relationship with God, I have been fortunate to have had a fairly instinctive sense that my Christian walk with God was about relationship, and that God has accepted my variations and weaknesses – even in the context of Christian/church expectations. I am not entirely sure why this is the case, but my character has allowed me to feel God's presence and to aim for reality and honesty. Before RW, both [my wife] Ceri and I have found prayer to be a powerful experience, and have sought and found retreats soul-refreshing – especially after discovering Ffald-y-Brenin,[10] a retreat centre in Pembrokeshire – but from our student days, where we ran many weekends away, we have known the power of being renewed. We have also sought to find renewal through Scripture and have experienced inner revival through friends and each other as we have talked and prayed together.

So, all this is to say that RW has given a structure, overall framework and language for a way of being which I had longed for but often lost sight of. Ceri and I would not have termed this 'wellbeing', so this has been the revelation for us that allows our natural inclinations to accept this and to aim to go deeper – perhaps to greater release from our learned 'forced rhythms'[11] of grace.

I acknowledge that our backgrounds and professional lives have made us sympathetic to issues of brokenness – from my years from 1987 in Social Work and from Ceri's training and practise as a psychiatric nurse, carer, learning support helper then teacher for children with significant additional needs. Nonetheless, there was much about these worlds which we did not reveal; in many ways, I would not have dared to reveal what I had been dealing with day-by-day because it would have been overwhelming for most people – but that meant that I was carrying a deep secular/spiritual divide inside of me. I didn't really know what to do with this. Some have managed to find a way of linking such work into their church life practice, but I was probably too bruised by it [which meant] that I had little to give. So, I stuck to the standard roles of youth leadership, music, church administration and leading small groups – many of which were good and healthy, but not wholly who I was in my completeness.[12]

We are so grateful to God to have Jonathan as part of the Renew team. His Renew Wellbeing journey started long before the first Renew centre was even thought of. This is a couple who were searching for a language and rhythm to allow them to be completely themselves, and when they heard about Renew Wellbeing, it just confirmed what God was already doing. The thing I admire most in Jonathan is his commitment to an honest journey, and to prayer and worship as the key to wellbeing. This story is one of homecoming, I think.

Time to connect
To help us connect in new ways as church, here are a few ideas you may want to use in your communities and groups of church that meet. Here are three ways to engage around this story of Jesus with those you connect

with. If you don't have anyone to be church with, there are thousands in the UK to choose from. None of them are perfect, but all of them have some folk who may want to share this journey with you. If it really is just you, you can use these ideas on your own while you think about who to invite to share them with you.

Be present: To use on your own
Read the story of the wedding in Cana slowly.

Read it again. This time, taking notice of the word or phrase or part of the story which jumps out at you.

Read it a third time, pausing and highlighting the chosen part.

Sit quietly, and ponder this part, maybe keep turning the phrase or sentence over and over while going for a walk or doing an activity.

Be prayerful: To use as the basis for a retreat
Take the phrase or word or part of the story and repeat it over and over.
Maybe close your eyes and use your breathing to help you bring all your thoughts to these few words.

Thank God for his character as you understand it. Name characteristics of God.
Imagine yourself in the story and have a chat with Jesus about what you see and feel.

Think of an event or ordinary day, maybe today, and picture Jesus in that day with you, in detail.

Picture the religious practices you have as empty water jars, and invite Jesus to fill them with new wine.

You could use this story as the basis for a retreat day, if you would like to. On your own or with a group, there are many retreat centres[13] and quiet spaces around the country, and giving a whole day to immerse yourself in God's presence through a story like this is very powerful. Here is a rough idea of how that day might look in case you are planning to open up the idea to others and are new to organizing retreats.

Start the day with morning prayer.[14]

Take time to read the passage slowly several times.

Give each person a copy of the passage and pens, etc.

Take some time on your own to select the part that you will meditate on.

Get back together and demonstrate meditation.[15]

Provide activities for those who might find the silence tricky.

Make it clear which areas are for chatting and which are for silence.

Get back together for lunchtime prayer.[16]

Take time in the afternoon to journal or do an activity that invites Jesus into your ordinary life. Take a good look at any identity issues that you may have with God, yourself and the church.

Come back together to share which parts of the story have been most important if anyone wants to and to pray end of day prayer.

Take the meditation 'Do whatever he tells you' as you leave.

Be in partnership: To use in a group or gathering
Discuss which part of the story you have been meditating on and why.

Chat about ordinary moments and decide to pray for each other through them. (Do a 'This time tomorrow I will be . . .' or 'A day in the life of . . .'-type sharing.)

Plan a get-together over food and invite some friends. Invite Jesus to be present at the event and then enjoy! Maybe it could be something that blesses your community with a 'best until last'-type give away: not wine, I suggest!

If you want to use these ideas in a more regular-style gathering or all-age service, maybe try some of the ideas below (NB. This is *not* a Renew Wellbeing space which would always be *no* proselyting, and any faith and none. This is a way of using the style of Renew to gather and learn together as God's people, which could also be a better way for unchurched folk or those who struggle with anxiety to engage with church.)

- Set up your worship area in a Renew style, i.e. some tables for activities, a quiet space for prayer and a 'help yourself' refreshments zone.

- Invite people to listen to the story being read several times.
- Give people copies of the text and highlighters so they can choose the bit that speaks to them.
- Get into groups to discuss, but also provide activities on the tables for those who find discussions scary. Always have the quiet space available for anyone who wants to just be on their own with God.
- In the activities you could maybe: make jars out of clay that represent your ordinary lives, make some good drinks to share (not alcohol, as it can be really hard for those who have an issue with addiction), have some colouring sheets with aspects of the story, have a 'Do whatever he tells you' table to pray, discuss things that God is saying to people, or any number of other creative ways of engaging. Work with the group you have. Some prefer quieter activities with more guidance, some are happy to have a go at something challenging or new. Make sure there is choice and it is clear how to choose. Make it as simple to set up as possible and invite all to play their part, not just you doing all the work.
- Gather together for simple prayers and songs of worship in whatever style you use. Thank God for his character as seen in Jesus. Bring the jars and place them on a table. Invite God to fill them and then invite folk to take them away again as you leave as symbols of pouring out the best wine in our everyday lives and encounters.

Blessing

Do whatever he tells you

Trust him
Even though you aren't sure you really know him
Listen to him
Even though the sound of your own plans is so loud
Look at him
Even though there are so many other options trying
to catch your gaze

He is the wine-making, face-saving, party-staying
Type of Saviour
He is the kind, listening, responsive, 'with you'
Type of friend
He is the extravagant, giving, lavish
Kind of lover
He is the One you should invite to the event
Before the others

This Son of God knows how to turn the very ordinary into red-letter days
This God made flesh knows how to refill with life,
our old religious ways

This man of sorrows knows how to save the best
for last
He is present, he is our future and he can redeem
the past

Do whatever he tells you

Economy: Measuring Value and Worth

Learning the value of one

To live lives of wellbeing and become communities of wellbeing, I am learning that the old ways of measuring success and avoiding failure will have to go. This wellbeing culture has an altogether different economy than the measures we have been using to fill our diaries and run our churches.

> THOUGHT: The measures I use do matter.
> QUESTION: How are we measuring wellbeing?

Connecting with my story: Learning a new measuring system

After my idyllic yet hero-obsessed childhood, I went to university full of the right answers, or so I thought, for how to be a successful Christian. This was going to be hard work and sacrifice but I had read the book several times, memorized the key verses and had lots of people telling me I was a good Christian girl. I had used my summer holidays to serve God in a variety of ways, including beach missions and overseas trips, and my weekends to be a seriously professional churchgoer. There is nothing at all wrong with these pursuits, please don't misunderstand me; they probably kept me out of all sorts of trouble, which may well have been the point of them.

I also learned loads from those who faithfully poured out their lives and gave their time serving others. But I built a few pedestals and placed a few modern-day heroes up there so I could keep checking my progress against their holy self-giving. To add to this, I read lots of autobiographies of great heroes of the faith who went, mostly overseas, and changed people's lives (sometimes they even did this in helpful and non-patronising ways) and the pedestal collection grew.

By the time I had become a grown-up (although some who know me may question whether that has happened yet), I had developed a way of measuring my success or failure, my performance as a human, that was not terribly healthy.

The measuring system went something like this:

- Have I been as much like Jesus as possible and helped everyone I can to the best of my ability?
- Have I spent enough time reading the Bible and praying today, and used my hours to do good and to be helpful?
- Has God used me to speak to someone else and change someone else's life?

The answer to all three questions was nearly always:
No of course not!
Try harder!
These were measures of:

• Success
• Time usage
• Usefulness

This seemed to be a reasonable way to measure my value as a human being, after the study I had done and the messages I had picked up along the way of following a God who would like me to be a successful Christian who used their time well to help others and to change the world.

My student years were actually quite good fun considering I never went near a bar or a drop of alcohol and spent my spare time at church or Christian Union. My desire to remain unsullied by 'the world' drove me. I'm thinking my life was more fun for me than those I tried to 'help'. I did make some amazing friends who are still friends today but even then, I tried to make sure I dragged as many conversations as I could round to which church we should go to and how we could bring as many friends to faith as possible. Again, it kept me out of trouble and the people I met along the way were often generous, authentic and loving.

It was the lack of deep learning going on in my own life in that season that I now think contributed to an unhealthy set of measures that I carried into my adult life. Learning was all head knowledge. I had very few tools to help me learn how to be healthily me. Tools like self-compassion and asking good questions about my own attitudes and behaviour were lacking. Skills like accepting help and admitting to failure were non-existent. Habits like setting boundaries and knowing when to admit I couldn't do something or needed help were not evident.

If the result of a successful Christian life was that everyone saw Jesus in you and everyone was pleased with you, then the pressure was on to make sure you made as few mistakes as possible and helped as many people as came across your path. If the result of a successful life was that you could go to bed knowing you had lived in a Christlike way and upset no one, then most days felt a little lacking in success.

The measure of time was also a key for me towards the 'less than peace-filled life'. Without realizing I was doing it, the value I placed on time well spent versus time wasted made me rush everything I was doing, as the next thing always seemed more important.

When I got married and became a mum to our three beauties I loved them fiercely and still do! But every minute of it felt pressurised and squashed by the minute yet to come. I hurried through a task to get to the next task until I finally sat on my kitchen floor exhausted and unable to even catch up with myself.

If time is a gift to be used wisely, then we mustn't waste a second of it with unproductive things, or so I thought.

Another measure that was unhelpful to wellbeing was that of usefulness. I talk in my first book about feeling like a spiritual spatula,[1] only created to be used by God. This was language that was popular in the church, and it still is. Bible verses like the one below are used as a call to be used and useful:

> Therefore, if anyone cleanses himself from what is dishonourable, he will be a vessel for honourable use, set apart as holy, useful to the master of the house, ready for every good work.
>
> *2 Tim. 2:21*

The word in Greek for 'useful' in this verse is *euchréstos*, which can mean good and kind, but is also the language of slavery for being used. There is no English translation of the *chréstos* part of this word that conveys usefulness and goodness and kindness all wrapped up. We see the 'useful' word again in Philemon 11. Here Paul is talking about Onesimus the slave, who he is commending being received back as a brother, not a slave. Here the words 'useless' (*achreston*) and 'useful' (*euchréston*) are employed to labour the point that slaves get *used* like objects. This is set against the language Paul engages in, of 'child' (v. 10), 'beloved brother' (v. 16) and a person who is 'my very heart' (v. 12).

Sometimes Ephesians 2:10 is quoted as a passage that supports the idea of us being objects used in God's plan. But the original wording here suggests we are God's 'workmanship' or masterpiece and that there are good works 'prepared beforehand' for us. Far from being used like an object, I have embraced this verse now to celebrate fully that I am made on purpose with loving hands and am still being made into the masterpiece only he can see. There are things planned and purposed that my character and gifting is best suited to, and far from being a verse that should drive us to work harder to try to do these things, I now find this to be a freeing and wonderful call to remain in the hands of the One who knows and made me and will partner with me as I find the things that best fit the shape of me.

But I had logged these verses early on in my Christian walk and stretched them out into a strict measuring rod for my own usefulness to God. This measure brought me problems when I felt less than well, less than 100 per cent.

If being useful to God was the best measure of my worth and if I gauged this usefulness by how many people I had helped, how many meetings I had attended or taken, or by how many times God had picked me to be his mouthpiece or his hands to help, then I was destined for weariness at the very least.

Being successful, using time well and being useful made for me a measuring stick that served a dual purpose, as a rod to beat myself up with when I failed to measure up to the standards that I had set myself that were not realistic for any human being.

The language we use matters. The measures we use matter even more.

The problem with being harder on ourselves than God is on us, is that we will extend that same judgement to others around us without even meaning to.

My student years and early married years, as I look back on them, cause me to smile and sigh. I thought I had it all tied down; I thought I knew God so well, and all I had to do was be the very best version of me and please him with my whole life and all would be well. Along with this 'hard to swallow' meal, I would have a side of trying as hard as I could to persuade as many people as possible to join in this exhausting way of being – or rather it was 'welldoing'.

So, this next Jesus story has become a firm favourite of mine in my recovery and new grasp of what measures we need to use. Come with me as I follow Jesus into his encounter with the woman at the well in John 4. Here we will meet with a new way to measure success, time management and usefulness. We may even develop a new way to measure wellbeing.

Connecting with his story: And the other's story
This is a beautiful encounter of Jesus with just *one* person, one woman, who culturally, he should not even have been spending time with. Here as we sit either side

of the well and put ourselves in Jesus' shoes and then in this woman's shoes, we will see a whole new economy, a new set of measures.

The woman at the well
Read this longish story slowly:

> Now when Jesus learned that the Pharisees had heard that Jesus was making and baptizing more disciples than John (although Jesus himself did not baptize, but only his disciples), he left Judea and departed again for Galilee. And he had to pass through Samaria. So he came to a town of Samaria called Sychar, near the field that Jacob had given to his son Joseph. Jacob's well was there; so, Jesus, wearied as he was from his journey, was sitting beside the well. It was about the sixth hour.
>
> A woman from Samaria came to draw water. Jesus said to her, 'Give me a drink.' (For his disciples had gone away into the city to buy food.) The Samaritan woman said to him, 'How is it that you, a Jew, ask for a drink from me, a woman of Samaria?' (For Jews have no dealings with Samaritans.) Jesus answered her, 'If you knew the gift of God, and who it is that is saying to you, "Give me a drink," you would have asked him, and he would have given you living water.' The woman said to him, 'Sir, you have nothing to draw water with, and the well is deep. Where do you get that living water? Are you greater than our father Jacob? He gave us the well and drank from it himself, as did his sons and his livestock.' Jesus said to her, 'Everyone who drinks of this water will be

thirsty again, but whoever drinks of the water that I will give him will never be thirsty again. The water that I will give him will become in him a spring of water welling up to eternal life.' The woman said to him, 'Sir, give me this water, so that I will not be thirsty or have to come here to draw water.'

Jesus said to her, 'Go, call your husband, and come here.' The woman answered him, 'I have no husband.' Jesus said to her, 'You are right in saying, "I have no husband"; for you have had five husbands, and the one you now have is not your husband. What you have said is true.' The woman said to him, 'Sir, I perceive that you are a prophet. Our fathers worshipped on this mountain, but you say that in Jerusalem is the place where people ought to worship.' Jesus said to her, 'Woman, believe me, the hour is coming when neither on this mountain nor in Jerusalem will you worship the Father. You worship what you do not know; we worship what we know, for salvation is from the Jews. But the hour is coming, and is now here, when the true worshippers will worship the Father in spirit and truth, for the Father is seeking such people to worship him. God is spirit, and those who worship him must worship in spirit and truth.' The woman said to him, 'I know that Messiah is coming (he who is called Christ). When he comes, he will tell us all things.' Jesus said to her, 'I who speak to you am he.'

John 4:1–26

I have reflected on this story in the chapter 'O is for One' in the *A–Z of Wellbeing*.[2] You may be wondering if I've even read the rest of the Bible. I have! But there are a few life passages, aren't there, that just keep calling you back into them. This is one of mine. This is a story I heard often as child but the new layers to what Jesus is teaching me are rich and varied. I bring you this passage again for a deeper dive in this book, and hope that it gives you permission to have a few favourite stories of your own that keep on forming and reforming you. We allow our children to read and re-read their favourite stories and in doing so, they learn so much. Let's afford ourselves the same childlike luxury of repetition. Here are some of my thoughts from the *A–Z of Wellbeing*:

He first asks her for a drink. This again would be unheard of. He is risking his reputation right there. But he chooses to come in vulnerability, in need, empty-handed, and ask for what she can help him with. No other man has treated her like this.

We gain so much from this attitude in our Renew spaces. Coming empty-handed, not in power, and having room to receive the gift of the other, honouring what each other carries.

Then he engages in theological debate with her and answers her questions. Most religious leaders would never engage with a woman in this way, let alone a Samaritan woman. Here Jesus treats her with respect and honour.

Then he appears to point out her faults, her darkest secret, as he asks her to fetch her husband and says what he knows of her difficult relationship history. But I don't see judgement in what Jesus says here. I see him telling her he knows what she is hiding, what she thinks makes her unlovable and causes her to be isolated. He says he knows and offers her 'living water' (v. 10). He is saying that he sees her and still accepts her. Maybe he is even saying that he knows she has been badly treated and he won't be one of the men joining in. He comes to restore, to bring hope, to bring life. She is hooked and runs to the town to invite the very people she was avoiding to 'Come, see a man' (v. 29) who she has found something different in.

That one encounter with one woman that Jesus went out of his way for would not be the way we might set up an evangelistic campaign to reach great numbers. But through this one woman, many would come to faith (v. 39). I tend to believe it was not even that strategic. I like to think Jesus felt his time was well spent just being with the one.[3]

This is a wonderful 'economy of one' encounter. One life matters to Jesus. Time spent with one person is not time wasted.

If Jesus were using my measures of success from my early adulthood, he would never have had this encounter at all.

- Success: in a public ministry spanning just three and a bit short years, we would never recommend this type of encounter. It is unproductive and ineffective and it would be much better to gather a group of influential people and deliver the message all at once.

- Time: far too long is spent just sitting and being present to just one person when there are many others needing help, or actually that time could have been spent resting and not being present to anyone to get energy levels back up and ready for the big ministry moments.
- Usefulness: this woman was not a person of influence. She was not well respected and she was a woman in a society that didn't value women. Not a good choice of conduit for an important message. Not very useful.

So, you can see why the younger me preferred the stories of battles won and heroes made. This Jesus way of being didn't fit my criteria for a well spent life of welldoing. Some of the stories fitted my measures better, but this one seemed odd and wasteful. Until, that is, I was the woman at the well. This story become a firm favourite when I was the one feeling isolated and misunderstood, when I was the one feeling I'd failed, when I was the one going to draw lonely, unsatisfactory water at the well of my daily life.

When I heard the voice of Jesus asking me to spend time with him, telling me that he knew all about me and still loved me, when that still small voice (1 Kgs 19:12, NKJV) whispered, 'I couldn't love you any more and I will never love you any less', this story became part of the theology behind that encounter.

Success, time usage and usefulness are not measures that Jesus employed to decide when to pause, when to spend time with people, what to do and be.

From this story and from my encounters with many folks who are not OK and need an 'at the well' moment, I am reflecting on these lessons about measures.

Learning from Jesus: When you are weary sit down and spend time with the one

One of the very first phrases I noticed here is 'he had to pass through Samaria' (John 4:4). Did he 'have to' go through Samaria – as no good Jewish leader would choose to go through unclean territory?

He had to go this way to meet this woman, I believe. I would ask therefore, where is our Samaria? Where do we 'have to' go for the encounters God has for us?

For me, the sphere of mental and emotional health is a place I have to go through; our Renew spaces are spaces of encounter.

For this chapter about measures and for the thinking about what constitutes a successful, well spent life I am reflecting on verse 6 which describes a weary Jesus sitting by the well. I noticed this for the first time when I wasn't well, even though I had read this story hundreds of times.

Jesus was weary!

We can sometimes forget that Jesus was fully human as well as fully God. He got weary. 'Weariness' is a word I can relate to. The trouble is that my old measures of successful Christian living drove me to treat weariness with contempt and push on through. I even thought of it as sin at times, proof that I hadn't time-managed well. I still struggle when people tell me I look tired or that I'm overdoing it. While well meant, it can make you feel you are failing to manage yourself well. I always thought weariness was less than Christlike; that somehow to be like Jesus we should be full of peace and energy and always pace ourselves well. But here Jesus is *weary* . . . like us.

It is what he does with weariness that fascinates me. He doesn't push on through, he doesn't even go with his disciples to get food.
He rests.
He stops.
He *sits down*.

Now, this would have been a radical way for me to live. This resting Jesus has much to teach me. This measure seems to imply that Jesus was aware of his body signals. He knew when he needed to stop, to drink, to be refreshed.

I didn't listen to my body at all. Many bouts of laryngitis preceded my burnout but I didn't sit down . . . I powered on through, as if there might be a prize for the one who never had a day off work; if not on earth, then maybe in heaven! (By the way, I particularly disliked during my time in teaching those assemblies that rewarded children for never giving in to sickness, the attendance awards: as if the children who had needed to rest and recuperate were just time-wasters and not deserving of a prize!)

Jesus then asks the woman to serve him a drink. He asks for help. He comes vulnerable and empty-handed and receives the gift of the other. Here is a very different way to measure the success of an encounter. In the Christian world, we would think it a successful moment if we had been able to serve someone else, if we had given up our drink to a thirsty, weary person. But Jesus here shows us how to honour the other by being honest about our own need and lack. The Son of God could have got himself a drink some other way, surely? But he chooses to allow the woman the dignity of also being able to give.

The encounter is full of respect. The time spent would have been surprising to this woman. The engagement in theological debate with a rabbi would not have been something this woman was used to being allowed to do. The statements about her past were not meant to judge and condemn, but merely as a statement that Jesus did know why she was hiding away from society and that he still chose to engage. He knew her and he still chose her. This was the point that she got when she later said, 'Come, see a man who told me all that I ever did' (John 4:29). She has been used to hiding her real life, being isolated by her circumstances and maybe mask-wearing to fit in. But here she is seen. He places value on what others did not value.

These are very different measures of success, time and usefulness. In fact, a whole new set of measures would be needed. I needed a new way to measure my own worth, and the worth of others too.

Learning from the woman: Pause and be present
But let's also sit the other side of the well. I am beginning to learn a lot from this woman, who in my past thinking I would probably have just counted as yet another sinner that Jesus helps. We can assume she has been badly treated by her community, and by men. She is alone collecting water, which would have been a very sociable daily chore usually, simply because her life circumstances set her apart from others. The many marriages and current living arrangements take place in a world where men held all the power.

Mental health journeys can feel like this – no two people are alike in their mental and emotional responses, and it can feel very isolating to have people misunderstand you, judge you or attach stigma to you.

Sometimes this is in our own heads; maybe it was with this woman. Sometimes we isolate ourselves, as we think people will not understand. Certainly, this was the case with me. I felt like people must be talking about me, judging me, thinking I was a bad mother, languishing in bed all day. This was almost certainly not the case. But it was very isolating. When we get trapped inside our own heads, it is hard to escape the self-abuse.

But instead of running away when a strange man at the well asks her for a drink, she stays. This is very brave.

She has kept on going to get water. She has not given up daily self-care habits. And here she is, risking being badly treated by yet another man so that she can give him some water. I admire her.

This is the sort of admiration I began to feel for those who were struggling with long-term mental health diagnoses, after I had experienced a little of what their life is like. I met amazing people who had spent years in and out of hospital, often being misunderstood and stigmatized, and I began to learn from them. I was in awe of those who were feeling much worse than I was, and for much longer, who were still getting out of bed, still functioning, still using their jar to serve water to others.

I was even more in awe of those who felt anxious and isolated but who kept going to the well, kept going to places they thought might help, like church for instance. Many of my heroes became those shadow people, the car park people, who stayed outside the building until the service had started and dashed straight out at the end. I began to understand how much it cost them to be there at all, and wondered how they did it. I had seemed unable to, and they were feeling much worse than I had.

My measures of heroism were shifting as my old measures of success, time and usefulness became obsolete. From this woman I learned:

• Keep going to the well, keep doing the daily self-care habits, even when you feel nothing and no one is with you.

- If someone asks for your gift, even if you think it's not much, be prepared to give them what you carry, to use your pot.
- If you encounter love, be brave enough not to run away.
- Pause. Be present. Engage fully with the one opposite you. Maybe you are meeting with God himself.

Connecting with our story: The church learning new measures the Renew Wellbeing way

For my own journey, I often need prompts to help me remember things that are character-forming and important. In this instance I have settled on the acrostic BE.

B stands for *bigger story*. If we need to measure the size of something, then let it be the size of the story we live in and are part of.

E stands for *encounter quality.* If we need a qualitative measure, then let it be the quality of the engagement with that bigger story, with the one.

Here are some stories from those who are learning new measures, who are finding the size of the *big* story helpful, and who are measuring quality of encounter in our Renew spaces.

Renew Sneinton: Resisting the urge to be driven by numbers

Emma leads Renew Sneinton in Nottingham and says this:

Renew Sneinton started earlier in 2023 and has been a real gift to hosts and those who have been coming along. St Stephen's has had words and promises[4] given of it as a place of sanctuary and peace, so Renew Wellbeing just fit that so perfectly, it was an absolute no-brainer to start a space of our own. The best thing is having people return each week and tell me again and again that they love Renew Sneinton, that they feel at home in that space, that they feel peaceful in that space and that they are so thankful to God for the friends they have made there. It has been beautiful watching people journey with faith in the prayer times (I am regularly holding back tears of joy from what people are saying to God!), and an absolute honour to have conversations with people about faith and hear all their thoughts and questions, as well as just being able to have nice chats with others and a laugh during the week. *The hardest part for me personally and, I think, for some of the other hosts has been accepting that the space is for us too . . . that felt really countercultural for a while and the instinct to be driven by numbers has been tricky to overcome, but reminding ourselves regularly that the space is for our wellbeing just as much as the next person to walk through the door has been super important.* Now I regularly have hosts (as well as guests) telling me that Renew Sneinton is the highlight of their week because they just get to be . . . and draw/knit/colour! It is the calmest yet most rewarding part of my week and is such a joy to get to lead our little space.[5]

I love the fact that Emma has spotted the economy of one. She has included herself in that one. Her phrase 'driven by numbers' echoes so much of what leaders can feel when starting any new venture or serving their communities in any way. I am so delighted to see this simple space bringing such joy. It is, in fact, the centre I attend for my own wellbeing, and I love it.

Bev's story: On realizing you are 'the one'
Bev set up and leads a lovely Renew space in South Wales and also is a Local Link[6] promoting Renew Wellbeing to others in the area.

I was first introduced to Renew Wellbeing and to Ruth personally in 2020 during the pandemic and lockdown. BUGB[7] were hosting a prayer evening each week. Ruth shared the ethos and beginnings of Renew and the prayer rhythms. Having suffered with anxiety and depression myself, this resonated with me and God touched my heart to find out more and get involved. I caught the vision even before reading Ruth's story in her book. I spoke with our minister at the time and the area coordinator to express our interest in opening a Renew space, which happened in September 2021. Fast forward a good few months, and I found myself overcome with anxiety and depression and needing to seek support from a social prescriber.[8]

At this time, I questioned my calling and passion to lead our church to open a centre . . . 'Lord, how can I do this when I am not in the best place mentally and emotionally and haven't the strength to take this forward?' I cried; I look back and see God's sense of humour to use someone clinically depressed to lead a wellbeing group. This is mirrored in Ruth's own story in part. *We talk about 'the one' – I believe I was the one to take a lead* and those who came are the ones who have helped me through my wellbeing journey, and me in theirs, and this continues. It's by his strength that I jointly lead this work and there have been many, many days he has carried me, and still does. He goes before me and is always a present help. I feel honoured and blessed to be involved in Renew Wellbeing and to be a daughter of the King of kings. All praise, honour and glory to him.

May God's favour be upon you and establish the work of your hands.[9][10]

It is such a humbling thing to read this and see the courage Bev has to have a go, to believe that our brokenness is already known to God and he still calls us. It is a delight to get to know people like Bev, who may well have discounted themselves from involvement in many church-based activities and have become isolated in their mental health struggles. Seeing broken folk realize they can be the very thing that lets the light out is always a beautiful moment for me.

Naomi is our coordinator for Wales and has encouraged Bev in her role as a Local Link. She says this about how she is learning to measure success differently:

Part of the joy of my job as a coordinator is hearing all the stories coming out of the Renew spaces in Wales and the impact they are having on individual lives. As I go around and visit spaces and sit and chat with regulars, similar themes get shared. People who were lonely have found companionship, people who were feeling isolated have found a place to belong, people feel 'seen' and valued and appreciated. Within the context of church, it's very easy to judge how well things are going by the number of people who attend, but it's so refreshing to feel the success of these spaces based on the warmth, love and generosity they exude – *to base our success criteria on the transformation that people are experiencing in their lives, one by one, because every single person matters. That's the Jesus way of doing things.* It's such a beautiful expression of the gospel in action.[11]

Shirley's story: Resisting the urge to 'work the room'
Shirley runs a Renew space and is also our wonderful area coordinator for the South East.

When you take on a role within the church leadership team you feel so privileged to do it, yet the responsibility of it weighs heavily. This comes on top of being wife, mother and daughter. Opening a Renew space has taught me so much about slowing down and being present. I gradually realized that I never really slowed down and hardly knew how – I was always telling myself I could do that once everyone was OK. The bit I hadn't taken on board was that that never happens! When we set up the Renew space, I would be constantly walking around checking everyone was OK.

I then started to realize that this was a space where everyone was on the same level. I don't need to make cups of tea for everyone. In fact, I could sit down and accept the offer of a cuppa from someone else. It was OK to look after my own wellbeing. Renew gave me permission to do that.

If we don't slow down, we will miss what he is doing in the room because we are too busy measuring our successes and failures by the world's standards. For me, what is happening in this Renew space is more exciting than anything I've seen in church for ages.[12]

Time to connect

To help us connect in new ways as church, here are a few ideas you may want to use in your communities and groups of church that meet. Here are three ways to engage around this story of Jesus with those you connect with. Being present on your own, being prayerful on retreat and being in partnership with others in a group or gathering.

Be present: To use on your own

Recognize where you are weary and *sit down*. Put time off in your diary regularly.

Take the John 4 story and read it slowly a couple of times. Highlight the part of the story or phrase that jumps out at you.

Meditate on or discuss/journal why this phrase has struck you particularly.

Be prayerful: To use as the basis for a retreat
Meditate on the phrase you chose earlier. Breathe in and out, and use the words to steady your mind and heart.

Imagine sitting opposite Jesus at the well. What might he ask you to give him? What might you ask him to explain for you? What might he offer you? How might you respond?

Imagine sitting the Jesus side of the well and seeing the other, maybe someone you have noticed in need. See what gift they carry for you. See them with Jesus' eyes.

Receive the living water he offers you. Maybe you could pause and make a drink, and drink it slowly as you ask God to fill you with his life again.

This could form the basis of a day away on your own or with others.

Be in partnership: To use in a group or gathering
To use this story in a group or a gathering, maybe think about how you will set out the space for smaller groups, almost around wells (little circles). Also, maybe think about making sure there are everyday things to do, like an activity to share. It can be easier to talk deeply when there is a shared task. The well was the place of everyday chores, so maybe this is a story to discuss on a walk, while doing some jobs together – gardening, decorating – maybe a shared task could help.

Having read the story, discuss what jumped out at you. Have options for those who would rather be quiet (colouring, art, jotting) and those who want to make or write instead of discussing (e.g. decorate a water jar, make a water container, or any water-based/container-based activities).

Try a 'sit either side of the well' role play if that suits your group, although that could feel a bit much for most people, so be sensitive.

Take time to encounter Jesus together and receive his living water in worship (you can simply listen to a worship track or spoken prayer).

Blessing

In all of this becoming
May you know the only good opinion you ever need
Is the One
Whose love you cannot earn
But who will literally bleed
With Love for you

In all of this doing
Pause oh weary one
Sit down at the well with him
He knows your soul
He's seen your sin

He's asking you for company
He's chosen you today
He's taken this path through your life
He's the Way that's come your way

And he will stay
And he will wait
And he will offer you
A cup you've never drunk before
His living, loving water
That will leave you full but wanting more

May the blessing
Of being at the well
Be to you
Wellbeing
Today

3

Community: Being Present to Others

Getting active with what you have, not what you think you need

Added to a determination to connect with true identity and beginning to learn a change in our economy, a third area I am exploring for my own wellbeing is that we can't do this on our own; that church really is a good idea, a God idea, and that wellbeing needs to be shared to be fully experienced. But church attendance is not on the increase, despite some encouraging reports about people's increased interest in spirituality. *Premier Christianity* magazine talks about declining numbers attending church and quotes the Brierley Consultancy report as saying 'that church attendance between 1980 and 2015 declined from 6.4m to 3m'.[1]

In November 2018, the Bible Society conducted research that suggested a strong interest in religious belief on the increase. A global pandemic may well have changed that of course. But the *Telegraph* reported a '50 per cent surge in online searches for prayer' in 2020 at the height of the lockdowns.[2]

My reflections are around the fact that even though people are not negative about faith, there is still massive decline in church attendance. What can we learn about being communities of wellbeing where people can discover a life-changing faith in God? Would this change of emphasis towards wellbeing affect people's attendance, even? Or is attendance at a gathering not the issue at all if church is something we are and not something we go to? Could our gathering together look altogether different if the God of wellbeing was at the heart of it?

> THOUGHT: Wellbeing is not just personal: we need community even if we don't want to need it.
> QUESTION: Who do you share wellbeing habits with in community?

Connecting with my story: Getting active in community

My story with community and a sense of wellbeing is a fairly positive one right through until recently. As I said earlier, my earliest memories are of fantastic family times, loved and secure. My sisters and I often squabbled, but it was because we knew we could and still get away with it, still be accepted and loved. We also used to go straight from a squabble into planning, designing and making a board game from cardboard boxes and sticky tape. You could smell the beach from anywhere we lived in the Isle of Man, and weekends were spent collecting shells, looking in rockpools and swimming when we dared.

I say that's how we spent weekends but in reality, a good half of the weekend was spent at church. It was quite normal to go three or four times on a Sunday. Morning worship, afternoon Sunday school, teatime outreach in the summer and an evening gospel service. Add in the communion after the morning service which had its own mini sermon (sometimes not so mini), the pre-service prayer meeting for the gospel service and the *Fact and Faith* film and after-church social, and Sunday was a pretty busy day. My poor mum usually invited people back for lunch. It would be a full Sunday roast, I might add. How did she do it? We were literally no help unless someone was watching who could praise us, which often happened, and our dear mum never shopped us. She always said, 'Yes, the girls are wonderful. I am so blessed!' You could say that was an outright lie, but it wasn't. My mother inhabits a world that is several parts imagination and more than a few parts prophesying what she'd like to see to be true. It is a more peaceful way to live.

But with all of that, my childhood was protected and full of love. The community of home and church felt safe and known. Our family was not just the people we lived with, hugged and fought with, but many and varied folk, like the old gentleman who prayed for so long out loud each week that we began timing him and taking bets. It was a rich tapestry of different ages and stages of life that formed community for me. And far from feeling trapped or indoctrinated, it made me feel held and wanted. It made me believe that what I did affected others and that my life might have purpose beyond satisfying my own needs and wants.

Mum and Dad took us with them when they visited care homes and did beach missions. They kept us in the room when they led Bible studies or had friends for a meal and a prayer. They encouraged us to go to kids' groups and youth camps and, living out in the countryside, they gave us lifts wherever we needed to go so that we would be part of a bigger group than the nuclear family.

I'm sorry if this is making you envious. I know the family thing is a really tricky area for so many. I know the church thing is too. So many times, the very people who were meant to love us and make us feel safe did the opposite and made it hard for us to see community as anything but toxic and painful. I wish I could transport you all into my upbringing. Mum would certainly make enough cake. You would be warmly welcomed.

You would also see that I am looking back with rose-tinted glasses, and there are probably things that would make you yell, 'No, Ruth, that is just not normal.' But it was *my* normal and it taught me to value a wider circle than just the immediate friends and family, and for that I am forever grateful.

It was, however, a somewhat narrow palette of choice. Mostly the people we mixed with believed the same as us already, or were those we thought might be persuaded to join us. It wasn't that we didn't care about others. We were just a bit busy doing church to get involved with anything else.

My other great love was horses. Saturdays were spent with my alternative community . . . the stable girls. Looking back, it was a clever wheeze to get the jobs done for free, but it worked and we loved it so I'm not complaining. We would be picked up early Saturday morning by the stables' owner. As many as ten of us, teenage girls, with time on our hands, would pile into the back of a Mini Clubman estate with the seats down, full of straw. No seatbelts. No health and safety. Lots of excitement. Happy, dirty and tired we would be dropped back off at the end of the day having mucked out stables, led children on pony treks, had a little free lesson ourselves and generally been unwitting but willing slaves for the day.

This community ceased to be for me when the church thing meant I could never progress in my riding on Sundays, and my propensity to fall off a lot factored too in my decision to quit. It is only looking back that I understand how much this little community was vital to my early years. These clubs we attend, these interests we hold in common, unite us. It was much more fun than owning a horse and riding by myself – or at least I imagine it was. But these communities disappear, as quickly as they are formed, with the ability or interest.

University afforded me the chance to deepen my love and need of others. I kept the bubble concept of my upbringing and sought out Christians and a church. Having found one that fed students every Sunday I stuck with it and took a few others along with me. The friendships were rich and wholesome and some survive to this day. These were good years made better by community. But the concept of community had narrowed even further to include only those I felt safe with, only those who spoke my God language, only those who agreed with me.

A year spent in France widened that concept a little, but I still managed to find a church and a lovely Christian family to adopt me, and spent lots of time with those I felt safest with.

Moving to Nottingham to teach I found myself living with a family who, although wonderful and Christian, were so different to me in every way I felt completely out of my depth. I had come from a safe little 'hat-wearing' conservative Baptist church to a pioneering 'swinging from the rafters' (or so it seemed at the time) church that met in a school and in homes. I met my husband-to-be that very first weekend in Nottingham. Love at first sight, really. But his churchmanship was so scary and different to mine I very nearly missed the adventure of a lifetime.

The definition of community had become for me 'a group of people who believe the same as me and where it feels comfortable to be'. I no longer believe this to be the healthiest community in which to have your character formed and to become fully human. But at the time, even moving to a new type of church felt unsettling and unnerving.

It was in Nottingham at this church, Lady Bay Baptist church, at the mother church, West Bridgford Baptist, and subsequently New Life Baptist Church, which was a merge of two of the plants that came out of the significant growth in the 1980s, that I settled into a community where I would marry, raise a family, make soul friends for life and become a full-time leader. It was in this church that I would have a breakdown, be loved to health and set up the first Renew centre. It was from this church that I would set out in faith to begin a prayer movement that became Renew Wellbeing.

It is this church, New Life Baptist Church, that taught me how to be community. With no building, we had to be the church, not go to church. There were meal runs when anyone was in need. There was a chance to raise children together, and share joys and sorrows. There was even a four-way house swap of sorts with no estate agents and lots of prayer that resulted in us living in the house we now live in. This was a group of people who got it wrong sometimes, like all churches, but they also got it very right. There was love and belonging. It was and is community.

When they embraced the idea of setting up renew37[3] before Renew Wellbeing was 'a thing', it was costly to them but they decided, and still decide, to put first the needs of those who feel most isolated and anxious. The sense of community deepened as we sat in our Renew space in the heart of our community and listened and learned from others who were not the same as us, who believed other things and nothing at all, who were made in God's image and were loved.

Leaving that church to set up the charity was one of the hardest things my husband and I ever did. But it was the right thing to do to make space for a new leader to flourish. We settled in a new church that was just starting in the city centre. A beautiful bunch of young people with a missional heart and the vision to grow younger leaders became a safe place to attend without needing to get too involved. These were lovely folk with great vision, and we sat and received after years of giving and leading. I had begun to understand that church is a wider thing than the local, and it was refreshing to experience a new way of being. The charity afforded me the chance to be community with so many wonderful folk, even if a lot of that was onscreen. Praying together each day became the anchor point for my spiritual life, and the little Zoom boxes filled with faces who became a funny sort of dispersed community who I might never meet in person, but who I felt connected to more deeply than some I had known for years. We spoke the same language and shared the same vison around wellbeing, and the connection was and still is palpable.

Within this change there has always been a small group I call 'little church'. Two dear friends and I meet infrequently in the home of a lovely elderly and practically housebound saint. Her home is the womb of heaven. Even though there are whole swathes of time when we cannot meet, we are connected in prayer, and when we do meet, the words and tears flow and we each feel loved and supported. There is a reason why Jesus said, 'For where two or three are gathered in my name, there am I among them.'[4] With only two or three it is harder to fall out, there is less to set up and the sharing is three ways only!

Beyond all the church-based family, the people I met in my teaching career formed a very real sense of wonderful community. The schools I taught in became my family. The colleagues I shared life with became great friends. We wept and laughed and played and worked too hard. The children in the class also became a community with shared values. We truly lived life together during the hours of 9 a.m. and 3.30 p.m. weekdays. The classroom became the living room for family to grow, for minds and characters to form. In many ways, a Renew space is like a good primary school classroom for grown-ups, learning to make friends and play nicely, learning to live well in our own skin and find ways to grow with wellbeing.

And beyond all of that is my family, my husband, Mark, and our three amazing grown-up children, their partners and our grandchildren, our parents and siblings and their families . . . all of whom make up a wonderful gift of a community that not everyone gets to have. This community takes up lots of our time and we give it willingly. They are such a delight and teach me so much about love and life. I am indebted to them. They are community, real community!

You can see that community, as something key to our wellbeing, has always been high on my agenda. It is for that reason that I find the state of mind and heart I am currently in at the time of writing so very concerning and disturbing. In writing this, I feel part of me is grasping how vital to wellbeing is the local expression of church, the group of people we share life habits with, worship with, pray with, reach out with, love through the hard times, laugh with through the joyful ones.

Three things have happened that have adversely affected my own grasp of local church and sense of belonging. Three things have brought me to this untethered feeling that has settled deep in my soul, and makes me feel a kind of grief for the carefree over-attendance of my early days.

1. The burnout I suffered made me view church through new eyes, which in many ways was a positive that led to the formation of a charity, but in other ways makes me wary of getting too committed, of giving away too much of myself, of getting weary like that again. Some of you will know that once you have been unwell, you walk with an emotional limp long after recovery has taken place. In some ways, recovery is always taking place. This season also gave me a hunger, a desire, for a new way of being in community that felt less busy, less pressured, more wholesome and peaceful. Renew spaces were never intended to be an add-on to an over-busy church calendar. In my mind, this was church being reborn into gentler ways.

   Yes, I knew there would need to be other expressions growing from Renew spaces. These simple spaces would always be any faith and none, always be 'not church', always be open to all with no agenda for church planting or church growth, always be simple places of prayer. I knew we would need to work out how to disciple, how to respond to the Word of God, to worship, to serve well. But if I'm honest, that was where I was heading: that Renew would be the defibrillator that restarted the heart of a gentler, kinder body in the centre of the community.

We talk about church serving the community, but I believe we *are* the community, or at least part of it. I believe that God loves humans. And we are also human. Renew was a way to place us back in a relationship with the world he loves to live out what we believe together. So, Renew ruined me for Sunday gathering alone and made me hungry for an authentic new monasticism open to all.

2. Secondly, the decision to leave New Life, the church we had loved and led for years, and to join a church where we wouldn't have to be too involved has proved to be one that brings me to this unanchored place. To have been a leader and then to find yourself not leading should be wonderful, but is in fact really hard. I remember hearing Adrian Chiles, in a BBC documentary[5] about his recovery from addiction and his renewed faith, say something about fame making people lazy. He talked about how you didn't need to try very hard as everyone knew who you were, and

when he wasn't in the limelight anymore, how hard he found it in social situations. I related massively.

As a leader who is no longer leading, I found my social muscle for talking to strangers had gone. I could do three laps of the room over coffee trying to pluck up the courage to approach a group and introduce myself. But I never did. I often found a lone person to chat to, but week after week in a growing church with only coffee time to get to know people meant that relationships rarely developed. My husband and I found ourselves (in fact, at the time of writing, still find ourselves) asking the unthinkable question every Sunday: 'So, are we going to church or not?' As if we ever believed church was a place to go to. What happened? Change happened. I was no longer calling the shots, choosing the direction, bringing the Word. I was not carrying the bread and fish. I had been emptied of power and I was unhinged a little by it.

3. The global COVID-19 pandemic had a massive effect on many people's church attendance and involvement, including ours. We went from over-busy programmes to nothing . . . overnight. This meant smaller groups meeting outdoors or online. I found this weirdly enriching, as we finally got to know a smaller group of people and we had more time free from the machine of church. (I realize the pandemic was different for all of us, and I ask your forgiveness if you were one of those people, to whom we are forever grateful, who worked right through with no time to Zoom or sit in

the garden chatting.) However, it wasn't long before we worked out how to keep the show on the road, and hardworking techies and leaders beamed the thing we called 'church' right into our living rooms, with various degrees of success and quality.

Those of us not making that happen sat back in our pyjamas and consumed church week by week. Some of us are still doing that, even though we might now put clothes on and go out of the house to do it. Where Scripture teaches us to come together and bring a contribution to worship,[6] we have translated this in a post-pandemic world into 'come to church and get fed and watered'. Maybe we always did this, but the pandemic brought it to our attention more, and some of us have not even made it out of our pyjamas yet. During those two awful years there was time to reassess how busy life was, and some had so overcommitted to volunteering and programmes of church that the relief of stopping has made us not want to start again. I believe few churches have used the learning of those terrible lockdowns to be church differently; in my opinion, most have returned to being just as busy as before, but in many cases, with a smaller core team to do all the work.

This all sounds very negative and depressing. I hope my story moves on, but my commitment to being honest and authentic requires me to tell the truth. I'm finding belonging to a body tricky to do, unless you count the Renew Wellbeing team and national family as church, which I do believe it is. But it's not local and it's often not in-person.

And I believe that is what is needed for church to be community that changes character to be more Christlike.
Real people.
Real mess.
Real lives in a real place with real shared habits.

I think we all know how vital community is for wellbeing. It is well documented and well researched that having friends, having people we love around us with shared life and interests, improves our sense of wellbeing.

The Campaign to End Loneliness charity reported: 'In 2022, 49.63% of adults (25.99 million people) in the UK reported feeling lonely occasionally, sometimes, often or always'.[7] The British Psychological Society talks of friendship as 'essential' for our wellbeing.[8] The Mental Health Foundation reports some fascinating statistics around the vital role community cohesion plays in people's mental and emotional health.[9]

This chapter is less about the fact that we need each other and more about how to be in community, and our community's impact on decisions to live well in our own skin with relation to our daily habits, how we treat others, what to say no and yes to, what to give and how not to overpromise.

Connecting with his story: Getting active with community
Community helps form us into more than simply individuals with wellbeing needs. The Bible would describe church communities as bodies, even,[10] where what one part does or doesn't do affects the whole. It is this sense of collective

wellbeing that I would love to look at through the lens of Jesus' wellbeing lessons in John's gospel. This time we are looking at the famously under-catered picnic in John 6 through the eyes of the different characters involved.

Jesus feeds the 5,000

After this Jesus went away to the other side of the Sea of Galilee, which is the Sea of Tiberias. And a large crowd was following him, because they saw the signs that he was doing on the sick. Jesus went up on the mountain, and there he sat down with his disciples. Now the Passover, the feast of the Jews, was at hand. Lifting up his eyes, then, and seeing that a large crowd was coming towards him, Jesus said to Philip, 'Where are we to buy bread, so that these people may eat?' He said this to test him, for he himself knew what he would do. Philip answered him, 'Two hundred denarii would not buy enough bread for each of them to get a little.' One of his disciples, Andrew, Simon Peter's brother, said to him, 'There is a boy here who has five barley loaves and two fish, but what are they for so many?' Jesus said, 'Make the people sit down.' Now there was much grass in the place. So, the men sat down, about five thousand in number. Jesus then took the loaves, and when he had given thanks, he distributed them to those who were seated. So also the fish, as much as they wanted. And when they had eaten their fill, he told his disciples, 'Gather up the leftover fragments, that nothing may be lost.' So they gathered them up and filled twelve baskets with fragments from the five barley loaves left by those who had eaten.

John 6:1–13

This familiar story of the feeding of the 5,000 can teach us so much, but here I want to look at why this story makes me realize what needs to change for me in relation to how I feel about community, and getting active in a way that will not wear me out again, but will involve emptying myself of all the preconceived ideas about what a community should do for me or I should do for it. This is a story that I believe shows us something of how to share what we have, not what we don't have. This story shines a light on what to do when fear of overcommitting gets too much. It is a story of how being part of a community enables us to experience a miracle of brokenness and blessing, rather than just eating some bread and fish on your own in a field. This is a story of how very much Jesus values the need for community and for sharing.

I want to look at the story from the point of view of the three categories of people involved:

- The boy who shared even though he didn't have to
- The disciples, who weren't that keen on the idea of a mass picnic
- The crowd that was fed even though they brought no bread

The boy who shared even though he didn't have to

Verse 9 tells us about this boy. He is the only one prepared for a day out, it seems. Everyone else followed Jesus to see some miracles, but no one had thought about snacks. If I was the boy, I would be a little bit irritated to have attention brought by Andrew to the fact that I was about to tuck into my packed lunch. I think I am quite a generous person, but when it comes to food, I can get quite tetchy – especially if someone says they don't want chips and then pinches mine! We have all been there, haven't we? A day out and no one except you has brought drinks and crisps, and suddenly everyone is peckish . . . and you're a Christian! Reluctantly you share, muttering about bringing your own next time.

But this is worse. This is not a case of having a bit less to make the bread and fish go round a few more folk. No, this is a case of handing over your entire lunch as 5,000 people want it, knowing that you will get nothing; well, maybe a crumb. This boy is giving up all he has with little possibility of getting anything. I imagine he is hungry. This is real sacrifice in my book – it's food! Maybe he had no choice once the disciples had spotted his lunch, or maybe he offered it willingly. We will never know. But this reminds me of every time the community needs seem to match the gift in our hand, and we get to choose whether to hide it or give it. I have done both.

If the boy had kept his lunch, found a quiet spot behind a rock and devoured it himself, none of us would blame him. How often we have heard of a need in the community or church that we could meet, and have hunkered down behind the nearest rock with a guilty look in our eyes and the faint smell of breadcrumbs on our lips? And this is not just local church rotas I am talking about, but the global church, indeed the global community of humans that we belong to.

When watching the TV becomes a guilt-inducing pastime, what do we do? There are so many needs out there, the news, the adverts for charities . . . How can we decide who to give our gift of time, help or money to when the needs are so great? What is our tiny bit of bread and fish going to do among so many mouths? I often have to turn the TV off when a charity advert comes on; how bad is that? I run a charity! But I can't just look without doing something, and we can't always do something!

I am not advocating helping every charity, meeting every need. But I suppose I am saying that when we feel prompted by God, or when someone spots the gift we carry, we can choose to hand it over even if we are left empty-handed.

If the boy had chosen the 'picnic for one behind a rock' option, there would be no recorded miracle. Chances are, everyone would have gone home and had their tea. But the amazing compassion and love of God would be a story lighter. The disciples would be a big lesson down on their character formation journey. And I wouldn't have this story to show me the way to hand over my strengths and weaknesses to the One who might bless, break and share them, and have my story become part of his miraculous story. The funny little idea to set up a space to be present, prayerful and in partnership was just for me, or so I thought. It seems God can bless and break broken things and share them too.

The boy may well have been embarrassed to hand over so little for so great a need. I know I often am, when I speak of how God is using my fractured little story to help other churches start something life-giving. I often say I should have called my first book *Is That It?* The look on some people's faces when I tell them that Renew Wellbeing is helping churches show up, put the kettle on, pray and do jigsaw puzzles is priceless. The confused expression when I say we don't encourage prayer ministry or counselling says it all . . . really, 'is that it?' How can this little bit of bread and fish really feed the hungry? But blessed, broken and shared, it seems to.

This is all we are being asked to do when we are invited to become part of the miracle of community. We are invited to give who or what we are. It may seem inadequate. Our gifts may seem puny and weak, or they may seem precious to us and we want to hold on to them for ourselves. Either way, the invitation remains. The choice is ours. The life that Jesus offers was never meant to be a picnic for one. The *shalom* of God is for all. If we hold something good, it is probably made for sharing in some way so that it multiplies.

We know this because Jesus showed us the ultimate way to multiply love; to see one life become life for all was to give that life up. We follow the way of the cross. We should not be too surprised when giving over what we think is ours to hold becomes part of how we see the miracle unfold.

I have another small issue with this story, and it's slightly ridiculous. You see, I can't bear anyone else touching my food. It's a family thing from my family of origin. We are all a bit squeamish about other fingers handling what will go in our mouths and vice versa. I was never one of those mums who ate the leftovers from their child's plate . . . even when it was something delicious. So, the idea of handing over carefully prepared and wrapped sandwiches to One who will break it into bits, hand it to others, who will then pass it round, appals me. By the time I got my share back of my own beautiful lunch, it would have been contaminated by so many hands. The boy must have been tempted to hand over most of it and keep his share untouched by others. But that was not the Jesus way of community.

It's a weird point I am making, but it strikes me that my current state of heart has a lot to do with this particular issue. My plans are carefully formed and wrapped for my day, for my life, even. I don't want my heart and my moments handled by others. I don't want to get too close to too many people and have their fingerprints all over my life. I have a few lovely friends and great family. They can break bits of me and share. But surely that will do.

There is risk involved in being willing to hand over who you are to be part of a miracle. The goodness we receive back will have handprints of others on it. The lone journey I take of deep spiritual growth and wellbeing sometimes feels too personal to have it broken and shared. I don't really want to share my time, my table and my toys. As I am learning to bask in the beauty of God's creation and the wonder of his presence in his world, I could be tempted to think it might be OK to leave behind the risk of others touching my life and to take a more solitary approach to faith. It's a choice that is there and many take that solo path. Many of my friends have left the church. Many have found deep ways to connect with the holy, to love God and not to also take the mess of belonging to something local, and I am sorely tempted to join them.

But no shared bread and fish . . . no miracle.
Others go hungry while I eat behind a rock.
That doesn't sound much like my Jesus. It doesn't sound like the way of the cross and it doesn't sound like his 'love . . . one another' (John 13:35) mandate to me.

I know many who follow a lonely, solitary path are very connected to their world and one-anothering in other ways. This is not a judgement on the amazing saints who choose a different way to live out their faith. It is an honest reflection of my own heart.
I need people.
I need them to share geography with me so that we can be in each other's lives in some way, and reach those around us with the way we love each other. I need people to help me get active well, to have good habits for my wellbeing, to see things from new perspectives that grow my soul. That is why I set up renew37 in the first place. I need people to pray with, eat with, laugh with, cry with. I need people to encourage me and challenge me.
I am still that person.
I don't function well in a social or spiritual vacuum.
I'm not sure any of us were designed to.

I sometimes have bread and fish to hand. If I choose to hand it over to Jesus, then others might get fed. I can only hand over what I've got, not what is needed. That is up to him, not me. The little I have can be blessed, broken and multiplied.

Or I can eat it myself.

It is still a choice.

The disciples, who weren't that keen on the idea of a mass picnic

The second category of people in this story is the disciples. I may be reading between the lines, but I'm not sure they were that keen on a big picnic. At this point, they have been following Jesus for a little while and covered quite a lot of miles. They will have realized by now that they have to share him, but I wonder if some of them had followed him hoping for a bit more teaching, a bit more input, a bit more personal attention. I could be wrong. Might be me projecting my needs!

So here they are on the way across a lake and up a mountain for some alone time with the Master at last. Sitting on a mountain would signify something to them. It would be a precursor to some significant teaching. They might be thinking, 'Here we go, we are going to get some divine input.' And then they see them: the great unwashed running up the hill towards them.

John gives no clue as to what the disciples were thinking. This is the storyteller full of love and compassion. Other gospel writers tell us a little more. All four gospels tell this story. It makes it unique. We get four ways to view it.

Matthew hints at the frustration: 'Send the crowds away to go into the villages and buy food for themselves' (Matt. 14:15). Mark has the disciples saying to Jesus 'Send them away' (Mark 6:36). Luke also records the disciples desire for Jesus to 'send the crowd away' (Luke 9:12). You could interpret this as pastoral concern for the crowd's welfare, of course. I think it is more likely to be frustration at having to share Jesus' attention yet again. Where was the rest time they had thought was about to happen?

Only John frames it in a kind way. He puts a positive, loving slant on it and doesn't mention the disciples' bad attitude. Bless John! I probably wouldn't have written such a lovely account. I do like this gospel. Be more John!

In all the other gospels, Jesus tells the disciples to give the crowd something to eat and probably sets them in a catering spin. In this gospel, he asks where they could get bread from. This is teaching. This is Jesus giving the disciples his attention. This is character formation class in session.

I wonder if the disciples understood this. They were following Jesus and he was teaching them, but not in the way a rabbi might be expected to. This was no dry or dull education course . . . this was life lived together.

The classroom became everywhere they placed their feet. Maybe it still should be. Maybe it still is.

However, quite possibly as church we have formed a different expectation of community and Jesus' following. Could it be that we have made this journey a bit static with lots of head knowledge and little footwork? I wonder at how we have, as church, translated this adventure of learning as we meet people on the way, of looking for him at work in every situation, of welcoming interruptions as rich seams of learning. Maybe what we have come up with is a meeting once or twice a week, some Bible reading and prayers when we can fit them in, a rota or two to serve the poor. This fits better into a busy lifestyle, but is it community? And was it what Jesus meant when he called us to love one another and to follow him?

As I read this account, and indeed every miracle recorded, my attention always goes to the disciples to see how they are coping. I put myself in their shoes and realize that without the benefit of hindsight, they must have wondered what on earth they had let themselves in for.

This story makes me think that they would have preferred a bit more 'Jesus time' than they got. Maybe after the event they would say that they were always up for a miracle, that they expected it. But at the time, it must have made their hearts sink to see the hungry mouths and know Jesus was not their private property.

Dear church, there is a whole world that God has made and loves. He made each person we ever set eyes on, on purpose. From what I have seen and experienced in Renew spaces, these folk who would not consider themselves Christian, who would not think of going to church, are still hungry for a bigger story. In every Renew space there are stories of people encountering the presence of God in the prayer spaces. Some come to faith, many are simply pleasantly surprised. But it has broadened my view of who the Shepherd wants to follow him. It is *everyone*.

I wrote a dream in the form of a poem early on in the Renew journey and one line says this:

> I can see a place . . . where God is not privatised into meetings.[11]

This is still the dream. Those of us following him closely, calling ourselves the church, making room, a room . . . making space, a space . . . for those who are thirsty and hungry and haven't brought a picnic, and for us to be able to spot those who carry a gift – the little ones who have prepared something to share. It is from these picnic sites of community that we can spot not just the needs out there, but also the gifts. Everyone is a masterpiece in the making, and it is not just the church with the monopoly on compassion. Co-producing is the 'mental health speak' for what we are being called to do here by Jesus. The disciples are being called to look around them for what is in the community, and to offer him that.

So often we look at our communities as a big bucket of needs . . . but what about the boy with the picnic? He was not one of the disciples, he was one of the people! He held in his hands what was needed for the whole miracle of the multiplied picnic to take place.

Where are we as church placing ourselves so we can really see what is out there, so we can spot the gifts and blessing as well as the needs? Renew spaces are one simple way to do this. There are others. I long for every church to pick one and stick to it, or we will forever be privatising God into our meetings. We will miss the gift carried in small hands and the crowd will stay hungry.

Please notice that even though the disciples also had no food to share, they all got loads. Those baskets represented the twelve tribes of Israel but in human terms, right there, the disciples would see that there was in fact a basket full *each* for them after the meal was done. This is a God of extravagance. Remember the wine from the first chapter? This is a God who knows our real needs. Look at the living water offered to the woman in the second chapter. Here Jesus knows the disciples were after their own feeding from him. They had wanted their own private miracle and they got it. In giving away everything they had they gained far, far more than they could ever have imagined.

Such is the mystery of the surrender, the sacrifice of following Jesus and of giving all we have to be part of something bigger. We end up staggering under the weight of an entire basket of goodness if we dare to join in the impossible.

They say that a problem shared is a problem halved. It is much better to share a problem than keep it in and worry. This doesn't always feel like it is true, does it? It helps to share, but we still walk away in our own skin. But most definitely a good thing shared is a good thing multiplied. This story teaches us that. It is one of the reasons why we took the decision to go for a strength-based approach in Renew spaces. Some skill is needed in dealing with complex issues, and sometimes our well-meant advice is not helpful. But our sharing of honest ideas for wellbeing can always multiply if shared. We have seen it happen.

The crowd that was fed even though they brought no bread
Lastly, we look briefly at the story through the eyes of those who didn't bring anything and were not expecting anything, but went away with full bellies and their heads spinning with what they had just been part of.

These people may well have hoped for a miracle, but it was maybe more of the healing variety and they were probably expecting to be spectators. To be invited into the miracle, to become partakers of the goodness was maybe unexpected. I think it still is today as people seek a bigger story and look from the sidelines at Christianity. But when they are invited into the love and take a seat at the picnic, amazing things can happen.

First, Jesus gets the disciples to ask them all to sit down. Some clues as to why he does this are given in the other gospel accounts. Luke 9:14 tells us that Jesus asks for them to be seated in groups of about fifty people. To sit would indicate something was about to happen, that they had been invited to a meal or some teaching at least, that they were not just spectators.

And to sit in groups means they would experience what was about to happen in community, not just as individuals. There is power in shared experience. It is harder to misconstrue and easier to remember when others tell the story with you. Jesus knew this. He did and does care for the one, the individual, as we said in the last chapter, but he also wants us to share this good news in community, in groups. It is good news for *all*.

Our experience has been, over the years, of seeing churches sit down together with their communities in Renew spaces, and discovering that many thought the church was a closed club. They didn't know they could come and experience the love and belonging that is on offer. We have found that to simplify the offer and invite people to sit with us, have a cuppa, bring and share a hobby and maybe even pray with us opens up a chance to enjoy the miracle of God's presence and peace *together*, rather than the church feeling they need to have their own picnic first and like mother birds, regurgitate the truth gradually to the few who got into the nest.

Many are hungry for the reality of a God who is loving and kind and present. Many don't know they are invited to be part of the miracle because some individual has hidden what they have of the gospel and guzzled the lot themselves, or the church has set themselves around Jesus like a box to keep the good news in.

Some are wary of a picnic offered that seems untouched. Some doubt the authenticity of a gospel and way of life that is pedalled and not practised. Many want to pray, but don't see us doing it and don't know how to join in. Many want to belong, but don't want the container we hold God in and don't want to have to fill their weekends with busyness and rotas in order to be church.

I wonder if it is hardest to see ourselves in this category. It is hard to be the ones who carry nothing, who don't help feed people, but who just sit and receive. There are seasons when we need to do that. If we, the church who say we believe God is good, don't sit down and tuck in, why would anyone else feel it was OK to join in? We also are the hungry crowd. We also are human.

What might happen if all the thousands of churches[12] in the UK, not to mention the 37 million churches world-wide,[13] made their practices of love and life accessible to all? What if we saw the crowd and made room for them, spotted the gift they carry, sat them down and shared what God had blessed and broken? What if we offered the little broken bits of goodness we have, even if we think it's not enough?

Connecting with our story: Getting active as church in Renew Wellbeing communities

Here are a few stories of where this has happened in Renew communities around the UK.[14]

Renew Cathcart

Caroline is our amazing Local Link for a large patch of western Scotland. She helps host Renew Cathcart, which is an ecumenical Renew space south of Glasgow.

> Wellbeing in Cathcart began for me in 2020 when four friends started to meet together, initially on Zoom and then in gardens, once four were allowed to gather outdoors [due to the COVID-19 pandemic]. We knew wellbeing was important in our community, but didn't know where to start. We met every month and prayed, but didn't know the answer. We did come to realize that being together was improving our own wellbeing. God taught us to be patient and wait for him to answer our prayers.
>
> Six months later, we heard that one of our partner churches had seen Ruth Rice talk about Renew Wellbeing and they wanted to start a space. They had the venue, but not enough people. God put us together because he knew that was how it could be done.
>
> We did our training in March 2021 and began to meet in September 2021 for six weeks, as though we were a Renew space already, and the hosts planned and prayed. We opened after October half-term in 2021. It has been

wonderful to watch our regulars grow in confidence, build relationships and help each other. Everyone, regulars and hosts alike, see this as a highlight of our week.

I am learning to let go of doing and learning to co-produce. I'm seeing that God's way of doing things is better than anything I can imagine. I'm trying not to fix others, just to get alongside them. I'm seeing people through Jesus' eyes and becoming aware of why he loves them. I've discovered that anyone can pray, and a lot of people want to do so when we keep it simple.

I'm overwhelmed how people bring their gifts to the group, whether it's practical skills or hugs or cheating at Uno! Most of all, I love the sharing. One person is gathering stories of Scottish lifetimes to help them better understand their university course. Someone who still finds opening up to others hard, came to the funeral of one of our regulars – not something that was easy for them, but they chose to do it and succeeded! I'm heartened by the regulars who've started coming to church. Not because we're evangelising, but because they want to spend more time with their new community. I was touched by the person who turned up one day broken because of a cancer diagnosis, but was uplifted by the prayer time. And now they come each week, or sends their partner to update us on their progress. This is a place where everyone can see God's love and compassion, and it is helping to strengthen our community. And slowly it is creeping into our churches. The language of wellbeing is coming into meetings and other groups that meet in the churches. The slower adapters are beginning to talk to others about Renew Wellbeing. And all because we have put this in God's hands. All we do is turn up and pray! Praise the Lord.[15]

I love Caroline's comment about co-producing. This is a word we learned from mental health services. It means to produce a service together rather than one person doing unto another. It is cooperation, but more than that, it is honouring to the gift of each and allows all to give and receive. It is a key lesson we are learning in Renew spaces, and one of the reasons I wish every church would open a space like this. It dismantles the power dynamic we can inadvertently set up as we try to help others, and in doing so, disempower them. This space is particularly beautiful as several denominations work together in unity. Wonderful.

Renew Slaynt as Shee: Health and peace in the Isle of Man

Sara runs Renew Slaynt as Shee in the Isle of Man. This is a beautiful space in a Methodist chapel. The space runs once a week, but the church building is left set up in Renew style all week. Sara says:

Slaynt as Shee is a Manx phrase meaning 'Health and Peace', and when we opened our doors, we wanted this to be what embodies our Renew space. I had longed to have a Renew space in Peel, a small community on the west of the island, since lockdown, but had wondered who would catch the vision with me to open up a place in our town. It was amazing that God brought two ladies I knew (but not very well!) and prompted me to share about Renew Wellbeing with them. One immediately responded with, 'So this is what God was leading me towards when he said, 'Go west!', and the other told me that she had been praying that we would have a 'Place of peace' in the west of the island!

Initially we opened our Renew Wellbeing space for us, making sure it felt right for us before throwing our doors open. We meet once a week on a Friday afternoon and have grown gradually to a regular-ish group of twenty-three or so. But it's not about numbers – it's about being a space for calm, acceptance, friendship and community at Slaynt as Shee. *What has been beautiful to see is how we are growing together*, watching friendships develop and people care for one another.

When we opened, we were intentional about affirming one another – we invested in some beautiful mugs, which have affirmations printed inside – as people drink, they are reminded that they are outrageously loved, or God's masterpiece, or . . . whatever the words are inside their mug. Those mugs have been the starting point for many conversations about how valued we are, and people will often choose a colour because they love what it speaks to them, while others take potluck and see what words of love are being spoken over them for that day. It feels like a blessing being spoken over every person in our Renew space each week that is just for each one of us!

Being a Renew space in an established community means that people know one another well already – it's maybe not quite so difficult to walk through the doors of Renew Slaynt as Shee for the first time, knowing that the chances of you knowing someone there are quite high. However, this means that I always have to say we are a quiet-ish Renew space as a result!

Everyone brings something different and unique to Renew Slaynt as Shee – we have someone who comes with their paints and canvases each week. Part of our ministry to this person is that we display their artwork in chapel for the week, and then they bring something new the following week. This person loves that we value their work enough to put it up. Someone else has motivated us all to help yarn-bomb Peel for the Secret Gardens event, so we're knitting, crocheting, making bunting, creating 4 metre high sunflower sculptures at the moment! We are also creating a community garden at the back of chapel, which is our gift to the people in our town – open for all to enjoy and look after, and one of the entries in the Secret Gardens too! It's a work in progress, but one person who visited Renew a few weeks ago asked if we could twin the Renew Slaynt as Shee garden with their community space in north London – I said, 'Only if we can mention that it's our Renew Wellbeing garden!'

One of the things I love most is how honest people are with each other – when they ask about one another, they really care, and when someone is missing one week, they notice and get in touch with them. At the end of our afternoon, we pray for every person by name, and several people have started coming into prayers, just so they can hear that each week. *Some of our regulars, who don't go to church, describe it as their church each week, not just because we hold it in a church building, but because we are a community where they feel safe, loved and accepted.* Even when my Friday mornings have been frazzled or busy, coming to Slaynt as Shee is a haven of peace, a restoring of calm and a gentle rhythm. The simplicity of what we do, the repeated habits, being vulnerable and honest with each other – that's Slaynt as Shee for me.[16]

I love this description of Renew, not least because this is in the land of my birth, the beautiful Isle of Man, and Sara and I grew up together in church as children. I love that the concept of church is moving beyond the place we go to and the services we have. This lovely Methodist chapel looks like a Renew space all week, with comfy sofas and fairy lights at one side and the gathering area in the middle with the chairs, etc. Even better, there is a permanent quiet room for prayer. It makes people feel so welcome when they come to anything the church does. I love this. I long for more churches to realize they are not the building and for God to refill those jars with living water that tastes like great wine.

What a Renew space teaches us about community

In a recent survey I undertook of our Renew spaces,[17] these were some of the comments hosts made about what people liked about their Renew spaces. There were more than eighty responses and all had similar positives. Here are three anonymous stories.

1. With the Christian perspective and church connection in mind, spending time with people I have known for many years but doing things we would not normally do together, e.g. play Scrabble, other games, colouring-in, painting stones, etc.

   Again, with a church connection in mind, to be with people without an agenda has been liberating and refreshing – appreciating each other in a new sense – very much as people.

   From the wider perspective, relaxing in a group context, is not something I find easy to do, so being an equal part of a group of people is helpful for me. There is no pressure in this space to take on a role – just a general mindfulness (as a host) about the time we share. Another very liberating thought and experience for me is the idea of being community where the barrier between faith and no faith seems to shrink. The 'wall' becomes permeable – as we take an interest in one another.

2. There was a vision for our church concerning nets; the need to be mending and tending. This was applied to our congregation, many of whom were tired and worn down. The vision showed us that we needed to learn how to care for each other well, build ourselves up and then cast our net into our community. Renew has been part of that journey and has met – in fact, is still meeting – that need within our own fellowship.

That has been wonderful. It's been great to see who has stepped up to host too. We have also had referrals from our social prescribers and are building strong relationships with a couple of people through that route, people who would not usually come to a church. The relationship building with our social prescribers has also been wonderful and unexpected. One of the greatest joys has been building a friendship with someone who first came to our foodbank distribution centre. This person was nervous, anxious, tired and careworn. I was able to invite them to Renew and they came along. They started coming to church too and a community café we run. We were able to signpost them to get the professional help they needed, and we have watched them blossom. Yes, they've had setbacks and might well have more, but they are a delight and now a well-established and much loved part of our Renew community and church life. This person commented recently that we are just like a lovely big family who are supporting them. I believe that God's hand is upon their life, and to watch his transforming power at work is a beautiful thing.

3. What do I love about Renew? Lives changed by loving community; we open the doors, the people who come in create a community who respect each other, learn from each other, are kind, give friendship, laugh together.[18]

Time to connect
To help us connect in new ways as church, here are a few ideas you may want to use in your communities and groups

of church that meet. Here are three ways to engage around this story of Jesus with those you connect with. Being present on your own, being prayerful on retreat and being in partnership with others in a group or gathering.

Be present: To use on your own
Read the story of feeding the 5,000 through. Maybe this is one to do outdoors on a picnic, or at least grab yourself a cuppa and a snack and find a quiet space to sit.

Read it again, highlighting the words or phrases that jump out at you.

Maybe choose which category you want to sit with, the boy, the disciples or the crowd, and view the story from their point of view.

Recognize what you carry . . . your gifts and strengths as well as your irritation and hunger.

Be prayerful: To use as the basis for a retreat
Meditate on the phrase you highlighted.
Imagine yourself in the story, in front of Jesus, and talk to him.
Maybe hand him what you carry, or at least talk to him about why this is hard.
Ask him what he sees when he looks at the crowd; tell him what you see.

Take the offered bread and fish, the truth or goodness he holds out to you.

Collect up the leftovers by pondering on what you have learned from the story.
Eat and be thankful.
This could form a lovely retreat day for individuals or a group with shared times involving real picnics.

Be in partnership: To use in a group or gathering
In a group, this is one that needs you to be on picnic rugs or around picnic tables with bring and share food, bring and share activities, bring and share everything (not necessarily outside).

If this is in a church service, try to set up the space so everyone has a place to get involved and to bring and share something if they want to. Make sure there is always an escape space, a quiet space for those who struggle with change, and that this is made clear from the start. Choice is key here to make all feel at home.

Read or enact the passage. Talk about who you identify with most and why. Have activities for those who don't want to chat, like preparing picnic food or making picnic rugs or baskets, baking bread, etc.

Use the worship time to encourage all to bring and share something if they feel able to: a song, a reading, a prayer, a drawing, to kneel, to sit quietly . . . to honour the gifts shared and not worry when we come empty-handed.

Blessing

You don't have to always be the one
To bring the bread
You can sometimes be the one
Who just receives instead

You don't always have to be the one
who has enough
It's OK to sometimes be the one
Who can admit
When times are tough
That what you need
Is what you haven't got
That what you've learned to expect
Is
Not a lot

You don't have to be the one
Who has to fix
And pay
May you be blessed to be the one
Who is hungry
Empty
Waiting
And may your need
Spark a miracle
Today

Simplicity: Habits for Fruitfulness

Taking notice of fruitfulness

If our identity enables us to know that we are welcome at the picnic of wellbeing, our economy helps us measure more compassionately how the picnic is going, our community surrounds us to enable us to understand what a picnic is and why have one, then this chapter will take a look at the quality of what we bring to the picnic.

The reflection that leads me to write this chapter is that our time would be better spent attending to the quality of what our life produces by having simple wellbeing habits we can share, than trying to produce results and activities. This will apply particularly to leaders.

THOUGHT: Better to bring and share a little good-quality authentic fruit than a lot of tasteless, overproduced fruit. Character matters, and it needs simple habits to grow healthily.

QUESTION: What sort of fruit is your life producing?

Connecting with my story: On looking fruitful rather than being fruitful

In some ways this is the very heart of all I believe about wellbeing. This reflection comes from the call I have felt, since being unwell, to attend more to the off-stage life than the on-stage life. I am in recovery from being an on-stage kind of a girl.

Having been in various theatrical productions as a teenager, when news got out about a new show being put on, I never put my name down for a back-stage role. I was usually after a lead role. I liked learning the lines, getting into costume and into character, being in the wings waiting, then getting the moment on stage to put together all I had learned and be part of something that brought entertainment. In my late teens I spent what felt like the best part of a year rehearsing and performing a key role in a period drama set in northern England in the nineteenth century. There were wonderful costumes with bustles to wear, and a very small cast. It was an honour to be a lead character, and as a result, I still speak with a slight Yorkshire accent!

As a primary school teacher later on, I remembered the joy of performing. My motto was 'every child has a right to a standing ovation', so I made sure the performances we put on each year showcased every child on stage at some point.

It was maybe not surprising, then, that I carried this through into the rest of my life. As a good Christian, I can learn the lines (Bible reading, loads of Christian books, many conferences, more sermons than hot dinners), put on the costume (smart church clothes, sweet behaviour, praiseworthy prayers) and perform. At home, I can make sure everyone thinks I am doing a great job as a parent, wife, friend, even if I am paddling very hard under the surface to be what people think is a good Christian woman.

I'm being harsh on myself. It wasn't all acting. I genuinely love my husband and family. I genuinely want to be at church. I genuinely love helping people. But putting together my issues about identity and my issues about economy, leading in a community was always going to be a slog. Like a long-running West End show, it had to eventually pause at least.

It was during my pause, my illness, when I could not care for my family, could not teach and run pantomimes, could not keep the church show on the road, that I began to take a look at my off-stage life more closely. It was my wise GP that suggested I kept resting, as in their words I had 'emptied my deposit account and current account' of energy, and if I felt I had anything in me I should save and not spend for a while. It took a complete burnout for me to realize that what happened on-stage for the few moments meant a whole load of work off-stage by the many. In terms of my behaviour, expectations and activity, it had become nearly all on-stage . . . what it would look like to others. So little of my time and energy was given to what was going on behind the scenes in my mind, body and soul.

Maybe a better image of this is to step away from the theatrical language; I don't want to overstate a case – not everything I did and said was an act! But trying so hard to be on-stage all the time was exhausting. Maybe the imagery of gardening and growth is more helpful.

I refer to this in my book *A–Z of Wellbeing* in the chapter on growth.[1] This is, in some ways, more of the same. In many ways, as I delve into wellbeing, there is nothing new. The principles are the same. But this is a deeper dive, as I am coming to believe that my wellbeing and, indeed, the wellbeing of all leaders and most people, hinges on this issue. Is it just above-ground growth we value, or are we making room and good conditions for the roots of our lives to flourish too?

Here is an example. I had a feeling, with my penchant for things to look good instantly, that gardening might be tricky for me. Up until the point I became ill, I had only ever done the quick 'looking good' style – that is, mow the lawn, plant a few flowers every now and again, and hack at a hedge when it got too untidy. Our garden was a playground for the kids, and we were always grateful for it, if not a little embarrassed by it.

So as part of my recovery, and having moved to a lovely house with a beautifully sculpted little garden, I decided I might try my hand at growing things. I wasn't good at it, but it was lovely getting out and having a go. After leaving teaching and taking time to recover some energy, I was eventually appointed to lead New Life Baptist

Church full-time. For a variety of reasons, I didn't get ordained or accredited within the Baptist denomination, but the church voted almost unanimously to appoint me to be their 'minister'; and in Baptist ecclesiology, I took that as God's call and my anointing to lead. The denomination was very supportive of the church's choice to take a slightly different leadership path, and our regional minister (who now leads a church with a lovely Renew centre) came to commission me at a special induction service. It was humbling, and marked the start of a wonderful adventure with this faithful little church.

To mark this occasion, I thought some gardening would be symbolic. The intention, with my generous parents' help, was to take a patch of the garden that had nothing much going on, and plant it full of lovely colourful perennials as a sign of the life that God was going to bring to the church. And as I tended it, it would remind me to care well for the church. That was the plan!

So, the first thing I did was buy the plants. Yes, I know . . . all the gardeners reading this are throwing their hands up in horror. I was a novice, remember. I really just wanted a pretty garden, a healthy church, flowers, new lives. I didn't really want to have to do the hard work of preparing the ground. Luckily my dad was on hand to suggest I dug a bit deeper before ramming the plants in a shallow grave.

So, I began to dig. And days later I was still digging. You see, it wasn't a completely untouched part of the garden. It had been lovingly made into a stream with a bamboo hedge at some point by our great friends and predecessors. I had let the bamboo go wild and the stream hadn't worked since we moved in. So, when I started to dig, I hit a layer of stones. Then sand. Then pond liner. Then carpet. Then more stones and sand. It was deep. And there was no actual soil!

To make matters worse, matted throughout this were the roots of the bamboo. If you have never planted bamboo, please don't! The roots grow fast and shallow, but they are stubborn and wrap themselves firmly round anything and everything in sight.

So, you might think I would get help, remove the bamboo first, make sure all signs of the old stream were removed and fill the whole space with soil, wouldn't you? You might think that if you didn't know me well. What, in fact, I did do was to leave the bamboo in place, dig as far as I could be bothered, chuck some soil over the rest and hope for the best. I planted my lovely colourful flowers and stepped back to enjoy the view. It was a short-lived joy.

After that first season of beauty the flowers, not understanding the word 'perennial', it seems, died one after the other, leaving a bare and straggly patch of earth. This was not the imagery and prophetic word I had been seeking to place in my line of vision each morning as I sat and meditated. It was disturbing, to say the least.

But my learning was this. We rarely have a patch of completely untouched earth in which to plant our lives.

Often there are other people's ideas and hopes, other roots and old ways of being that affect our plans.

The next year we removed all the bamboo, dug out as much of the old stream as we could, and planted hardy evergreen shrubs, which are still thriving. The roots needed room to grow. It was no use just attending to the on-stage show of flowers. The off-stage deep roots needed moisture and space. Years later we got around to having the Leylandii trees – that took all the goodness from the soil and light from the garden – removed, and my husband bought a pickaxe to deal with the deep, dry roots before we planted anything else.

It looks lovely there now. No flowers grow, but evergreens do and we keep dealing with the persistent bamboo that continues popping up to take its place again.

This story of novice gardening leads me to the reason for this chapter. For there to be flourishing of wellbeing, for there to be real growth and life, the roots need to be healthy. In my life, there was so much attention given to what flowers I wanted people to see that the unseen life got little attention, if any. The root systems I had in place due to my own – and sometimes other people's – values and beliefs needed dealing with before there would be room for real root growth.

The soil we are planted in as God's people is his love. So how can this story help? If God's love is our foundation, how can we do anything about the roots? I think I truly believed when I came to faith that God would do all the off-stage work and I would make sure the on-stage show looked good. It is a revelation to me to realize that God is more concerned with the root system than the flowers, with the character than the performance, and that I do have a part to play in making healthy roots.

Connecting with his story: The invitation to produce better fruit

Before we look at Jesus' teaching from John's gospel to help us produce better fruit, it may help to define what is meant by being fruitful. I think I always believed it to be living a life that looked like Christ, that saw people helped and saved and set free. I thought it meant that I pleased people as much as I could, and cared well and consistently for all those in my life that I had been given to love and care for.

There are many references to fruit and fruitfulness in the Bible, but they are often ambiguous, leaving us to decide what the fruit might be.[2] The only clear definition of fruit in the Bible is in Galatians 5:22–23:

> But the fruit of the Spirit is love, joy, peace, patience, kindness, goodness, faithfulness, gentleness, self-control; against such things there is no law.

So, the quality of our fruitfulness, according to these verses, lies entirely in our character, not in our performance. These characteristics are those of Christ, and can only be fully seen in human beings when the Holy Spirit of God is present and active. The fruit seems to be a work of grace and of God, not our own work. This is absolutely the case, so how can we then attend to the roots? Surely that's God's responsibility?

The Jesus way to better fruit

Continuing our exploration of Jesus' ways to wellbeing, or what to bring to a picnic, we look at John 15. This is not a story like the others I use in this book, but a piece of teaching that Jesus brings to his followers in the time leading up to his death and resurrection. As all last words, this is very important teaching. I know all Jesus' teaching is important, but there is something about the things you choose to say to people when you know you aren't going to be with them much longer that takes on special significance.

Read this well-known passage slowly.

> I am the true vine, and my Father is the vine dresser. Every branch in me that does not bear fruit he takes away, and every branch that does bear fruit he prunes, that it may bear more fruit. Already you are clean because of the word that I have spoken to you. Abide in me, and I in you. As the branch cannot bear fruit by itself, unless it abides in the vine, neither can you, unless you abide in me. I am the vine; you are the branches. Whoever abides in me and I in him, he it is that bears much fruit, for apart from me you can do nothing. If anyone does not abide in me he is thrown away like a branch and withers; and the branches are gathered, thrown into the fire, and burned. If you abide in me, and my words abide in you, ask whatever you wish, and it will be done for

you. By this my Father is glorified, that you bear much fruit and so prove to be my disciples. As the Father has loved me, so have I loved you. Abide in my love. If you keep my commandments, you will abide in my love, just as I have kept my Father's commandments and abide in his love. These things I have spoken to you, that my joy may be in you, and that your joy may be full.

This is my commandment, that you love one another as I have loved you. Greater love has no one than this, that someone lay down his life for his friends. You are my friends if you do what I command you. No longer do I call you servants, for the servant does not know what his master is doing; but I have called you friends, for all that I have heard from my Father I have made known to you. *You did not choose me, but I chose you and appointed you that you should go and bear fruit and that your fruit should abide*, so that whatever you ask the Father in my name, he may give it to you. These things I command you, so that you will love one another.

John 15:1–17, emphasis mine

Here Jesus is instructing his followers about how to be fruitful, about how to produce much fruit. But it is verse 16 that jumps out at me as I read it again. We are appointed to bear fruit that will 'abide' or 'last' (NIV) or 're-main' (NKJV). This is the Greek word *menó*[3] telling us to remain or abide in Christ.

It strikes me as unusual to have fruit that lasts. Fruit by its very nature doesn't last. It rots. It is seasonal. It has a purpose and then it is gone. The sort of fruit Jesus is inviting us to produce and share at the picnic of wellbeing in our communities is fruit that lasts. This is not an invitation to make things look good, to hold it all together for a little while, to have a little bit of peace, joy and love that lasts while others are looking, and then is spent. No, this is an invitation to a life characterized by the fruit of the Spirit even when no one is looking.

This is a description of what wellbeing might look like; a life that, regardless of the circumstances or season, is filled with love, can experience joy, has a degree of peace, is patient, is kind and good, is faithful, embraces gentleness and practises self-control. This is a life I would love to have. This is a life that looks like Jesus. This is fruit that is truly fruity. Is it possible that life can be like this? Surely saying it is OK not to be OK precludes this fantasy life of fruitfulness?

Is it possible to be honest, to feel your own feelings, to be truthful and authentic in a broken world and yet still have this sort of fruit that lasts? I think I am beginning to realize my fascination with wellbeing is because I would like my life to be an experiment in working out if it could be possible that abundant life[4] is for everyone even on the worst days. I want to be a guinea pig in this experiment to see if we can have and share fruit that lasts.

Until I was unwell, I think I truly felt that there was little I could do about making sure the roots were healthy; only the plant itself could be affected by my habits and activity. I believed I needed to try harder to understand and believe God's love by studying his Word. I believed I needed to work out his love by serving. I believed I needed to stay in his love by obedience and not sinning. I believed the church could show his love in many ways, but I don't think I grasped then how I could cooperate with his love, how I could share a deep authentic fruitfulness that did not depend on me and my much trying.

This chapter of John's gospel has become like a manifesto for my recovering soul. The call here is not to frenzied activity but to dwelling, abiding or remaining. The way to have fruit that tastes of something is to spend time enriching the soil, making room for the roots, being watered and letting the sun shine in. The way to have even tastier fruit is to let the gardener prune even what is good so that what remains is better. The way to be a fruitful branch is simply to be stuck to the right plant, to be more occupied with clinging to the branch than with what fruit might be popping out.

My observation in my own life has been that the more I pause, the more fascinated I am with the person of Jesus, the more I dwell on God's character, the less I try to be fruitful and the more I gaze and empty myself and ask God to fill my thoughts, my moments, my vision with himself and his truth, the more fruitful I seem to be in terms of peacefulness and patience and love.

Before I was unwell, all my habits were directed outward towards serving others, trying harder. After beginning recovery, my habits began to be more about deepening the roots of my own being into the soil of God's love, connecting with the source of life, emptying myself of clutter and busyness. It seemed like it would be a selfish way to live, less helpful to others, more self-obsessed. But it is turning out to be the opposite, I think. The more I choose to look at God's character, to focus on his love, to immerse my inner being in truth and beauty, the more fruit seems to be produced that I haven't made happen. The mystery of God's life in us is that he is the vine, the plant; we are merely branches and the fruit won't come by us trying to make it happen.

The trellis: Top tips for remaining, dwelling, staying

Thinking about what is happening in my own life, my attention was brought to a plant I have been growing that is just in my line of vision as I write. This is a Ceanothus plant. This particular one is a tall, tree-like evergreen plant with fluffy purple flowers in the spring and early summer. I love it. It is the first plant I feel successful with, and as a result, I have it in various forms all over the garden. But this first one I bought a few years ago came with a little arch-shaped trellis for support. It was about half a metre tall and the trellis held the branches in a beautiful shape.

As I watched it grow and tended to it, I made sure it had deep enough good-quality soil for its roots. That lesson was learned. I made sure it had good light and was watered frequently. That part of growing I had grasped.

So, I was perplexed when many of the upper branches, as it grew, began to die, to whither and droop. I watered some more. I enriched the soil around the base. But still the sad-looking brown upper branches hung there.

Eventually I realized what was happening. The trellis was too small for the plant. The plant had outgrown the support and needed a new, bigger cane structure to hold it in place, to give it strength and life.

The trellis represented for me the way of life we decide on to support our beliefs and to structure our days. The trellis can be what we have in our diaries, what habits and rhythms we observe. The life comes from the soil. The love of God in which we are planted is not something we make, but the trellis we support that life with is something we get to decide on. We get to decide how to live in the soil of God's love. The trellis for me represents a rule of life. The Northumbria Community describes a Rule of Life like this:

> A Rule is an orderly way of existence but we embrace it as a way of life not as keeping a list of rules. It is a means to an end – and the end is that we might seek God with authenticity and live more effectively for Him.[5]

Before becoming unwell I had not heard of this ancient idea of Rule of Life. If I had, I would have thought it was a set of rules and if I had embraced it, it may well have made me ill much sooner. But coming across the concept in recovery through a spiritual director[6] really helped me understand that just because I hadn't heard of it didn't mean I didn't have a Rule of Life. I did, we all do. It is often unspoken, unrecognized, even by us, but we make decisions about what we do based on a set of beliefs and values, and our life fills with a rhythm that if we don't choose it, gets chosen for us by the demands around us.

My set of values included pleasing God and others with my days, so my diary filled quickly with needs and my journal filled just as quickly with things I needed to remember and learn to make sure I didn't fail too much.

After encountering God's love at a time when I was doing nothing useful and realizing I couldn't earn this beautiful, fruitful peace, I set about dismantling the old trellis of expectations and demands that was killing the plant, and with God's help and the help of others, began to establish a set of habits that would support the life I lived in God.

Here are some of those canes that made up the trellis:

- Daily stillness and meditation on the Psalms
- Daily prayer rhythms
- Frequent rest and hobbies that brought me life
- Shared life with others around these habits
- Working from my rest, not the other way round

Instead of a set of rules that would not be helpful for my 'Am I getting it right yet?' mindset, I came up with three words borrowed from the Ffald-y-Brenin daily prayers:[7] *Simple, Joyful, Gentle.*

These three simple words became my daily trellis up which my life grew. I asked myself when faced with a choice, a decision, when praying through a dilemma: Are my ways simple? Is my worship joyful and are my words gentle? These three little words helped me as I navigated setting up Renew Wellbeing. They helped me put down so many good ideas that were not God ideas. They helped keep me true to the calling God had placed on me. They kept the plant of my life true to its roots.

A trellis can strengthen the plant, give shape to the whole thing and keep the fruit off the ground. The three little words of my Rule of Life in those early days of the charity and recovery definitely helped me to not get distracted in a world with much need.

Simplicity is key here. This particular Rule of Life has proved a little too simple. As this part of my life has grown and I have engaged with the other key principles of this book, namely how I was identifying myself and God, and how I was measuring success and engaging in the community.

Three Ps Rule of Life

These three simple statements are not only the values around which Renew Wellbeing is formed, they are also my new Rule of Life.

This is a Rule of Life, a trellis up which my life can grow, that other plants can grow up too. This can be a shared Rule of Life, and these seem to be the best sort if we thrive best in community.

Being present in my own life means that I settle myself at the start of each day with stillness and meditation into the truth of the phrase from the psalm and the fact of God's love. I then bring this to mind all through the day whenever I pick up a cup, which represents my life held in God's hands. In this way whatever I'm doing, whoever I am with, I am reminding myself that I am in God's presence. He is fully present, so I draw myself through simple meditation and mindful practices to become fully present to him in each moment. This will be a lifetime's learning.

Being prayerful means I embrace the rhythm of prayer of a psalm each morning, in the Lord's Prayer each lunchtime and the Prayer of Examen[8] in the evening, as well as chatting to God throughout the day and listening for his voice around me in others around me, in his Word and his world, and within me.

Being in partnership means I choose to share the picnic. I choose to come empty-handed when that is how I feel, and receive the gift of the other. In short, I choose to live life in community. I choose to work with others to care for the world God has given and those within it.

These three short phrases can then become shared values with a community. The trifold nature means more stability to each day. Learning to show up, pray to give and receive in community is the trellis that forms the shape of my days, keeps the strength in my values and keeps the fruit from being trampled on the ground before it is tasted.

As life grows and changes, our Rule of Life will need to change too. What fits well in one season can become restrictive and damaging in another. As we age, for example, we may need to commit less to doing so much and be more prayerful, more in partnership. Our presence may take a new form, or we may need to look again at the whole Rule of Life and ask God for new words or images to shape us.

Whether we have a trellis or not, we can still and will still be held deep in the soil of God's love. We can still remain in him. The trellis idea can help us, though, to allow pruning, to be less panicky about change, to know that loss happens and God is still present, to accept help and have habits that we can share when others ask us if they can join in with what it means to live with wellbeing.

To become the communities of wellbeing I believe a shared trellis as well as shared soil will help. Leaders who lead such communities will need to take time to attend to their own wellbeing, to think about what their values and rhythms look like, and to allow some pruning of those things that rob us of simplicity.

It will mean saying no to busyness.
It will mean leading from our lives and habits.
It will mean practising not just pedalling what we preach.

Connecting with our story: Fruitful churches and honest leading from Renew habits

I was relieved to realize when I began the Renew Wellbeing movement that I wasn't the only one who had spent too much time and energy on single season flow-ers and fruit. I particularly address this to leaders, as the pressure seems greater on us to perform. Barbara Brown Taylor puts it like this: 'My role and my soul were eating each other alive.'[9]

Here is one brave friend willing to share his roots story and an amazing poem that reflects how hard it can be in church-based leadership to produce healthy fruit.

Leading fruitfully: Jonathan's story

Many leaders have spoken with me over the years I have been sharing my story about how refreshing it is to hear someone being honest about mental and emotional health struggles. Many hide their true feelings and keep turning up and giving out week after week until they re-ally can't anymore. A friend in a senior leadership posi-tion within the church recently said the time between hearing someone might not be OK and them leaving ministry altogether is getting shorter and shorter. Many are finding the stresses of the 'job' too much and are opting out for a more authentic and gentler lifestyle.

Many are leaving not just ministry but church too. The back door is wide open even as people walk in through the front door. Is there a way to live more simply so that leaders thrive, not just survive?

Wouldn't it be amazing if God could renew our under-standing of the role of leading a wellbeing community? I do believe that is the way the church could be perceived if we were to take a good, brave look at how we live, at what is shaping and forming us, at our shared rule of life.

Could we be pruned and more fruitful for the sake of those in our communities literally dying of loneliness, for those desperate for a bigger story to live in? The local church is still God's plan A to show his love on the earth. If we could lead more gently from our lives, maybe the world around us would be more interested in our message.

One brave minister friend Jonathan told me about his life and ministry, his struggles with wellbeing, and wrote the following poem on the occasion of my visit to share the Renew story.

In his own words, here is the thinking behind the amazing poem:

> Remain in me, as I also remain in you. No branch can bear fruit by itself; it must remain in the vine. Neither can you bear fruit unless you remain in me.
>
> *John 15:4, NIV*

> Being human means that results matter deeply to us, but when our sense of identity gets deeply rooted in outcomes, we end up holding our joy and peace ransom to a set of imagined circumstances.

> Plus, I've discovered, it is very possible to live (and minister) that way quite separately from Jesus himself.

But Jesus has a way of drawing our attention back to the other end of the branch – our living connection with him.

'Why don't you just remain in me . . . and let me worry about the fruit?'
There's a refocusing in that that I need time and time again; a real freedom in there that is beyond powerful. It's life-giving.

Healing as the experience of 'I'm not alone in this – I'm not the only one – I'm not a weirdo' (though I'm sure my kids would disagree with that last one), on its own, it's not enough. A bunch of branches, however well connected to each other, will still die if they're cut off from The Vine . . . Those kinds of real relationships are vitally important but can never replace the essential friendship that Jesus himself offers us.

Because he actually wants us to remain in him.
He actually wants us.
The full, real, broken, us.

'Remain in me' is an invitation as much as it is an instruction. It all starts with him, doesn't it? It's his idea, not ours – his desire so much more even than ours at our most desperate. But it's a whole lot easier knowing there's something – or someone – I can never lose.[10]

Renew

When the muscles of my ministry strain and spasm
From unsustainable serving and insufficient Sabbath
Spirit of rich renewal, restore my over-stretched strength
You who make all things new – renew me, Lord

When the pulse of my passion for people is hard to find
Exhausted by exacting expectations, starved of the
oxygen of genuine encouragement
Lord of limitless love, restart my flatlining heart
You who make all things new – renew me, Lord

When Your call to Pastor and Your call to be a Parent and
a Partner don't readily mingle or mix
And the pulling apart of my hurting heart delivers devastating disappointments
You who call me first to be Your friend, reclaim my calendar and re-centre my compass
You who make all things new – renew me, Lord

When my eyes struggle to see as good that which
You have declared as such
When I'm tempted to call unclean the picnic blanket of precious people You've spread before me
God of vast vision, recalibrate my bleary reality, reinvigorate my weary
You who make all things new – renew me, Lord

When my schedule becomes a treadmill, I fear I can't
step off without falling

When Your church becomes my build, my baby, my busi-
ness, my bandwagon,
When I'm loathed to listen, and label love's lesson as lies
When I screen my calls or scroll past scrutiny
When my blind-spots black out truths too brutal or block
out beauty too bright
When my prayer life is permeated by only professional
appointments
When my heart holds so many things it's too heavy to
lift to You
And when I don't even want to want to want You
You who call me first to be Your friend,
God of vast vision, Lord of limitless love, Spirit of rich
renewal
Come restore, restart, reclaim, re-centre,
Recalibrate, reinvigorate,
You who make all things new – renew me, Lord

Jonathan Vaughan Davies, 2023

Mary's story: Setting the posture for the day

Mary is our area coordinator for the South West and
runs a Renew space. She loves prayer and people and
has been such a gift to the charity. Mary says:

> The simple habits have led to a new calm (ish!) personal
> centre which life can move around and take its cadence
> from when the day starts with the reminders to bless
> God, to be grateful, to bring people, situations in a word
> or a sentence to the healer and redeemer, and then to
> be crowned with his love and compassion: it sets the
> posture/expectation for the day.

*This idea of simplicity and sustainability has led me to
see the church in new ways too.* Not as a driven, busy,
draining, energetic, exhausting place, but a place where
the presence of God can rest with and on his people.
To take time, to 'walk' slowly and allow quiet space is
now my preferred option when we meet together. There
are issues with how this model fits with the 'have more
faith', fervent encouragements to enter worship, etc.
idea of church. Often in this approach not being OK in
any shape or form is implicitly and sometimes explicitly
seen as a lack of faith.

There is a lot that I have unlearned and am still unlearning
in terms of 'us' being the answer, rather than the quiet
knowing that God is the answer and that people can find
him in the simplicity of prayer rhythms. Prayer should be
at the centre and at the edges and the far margins.[11]

I love the fact that Mary is experimenting with these simple rhythms across her whole life and the whole life of
the church. This is not just a quick quiet time so we can
busily get in with doing church. Mary embodies a desire
for Renew Wellbeing to be a way of life and a blueprint
for gathering differently. Whether these experiments
succeed or fail is not the issue . . . the beautiful thing is
the heart of simplicity behind these words.

Pauline's story: Simple and profound practices in Northern Ireland

My journey with Renew Wellbeing has been a personal one as well as a journey with community. I was

deeply touched by Ruth's story, probably because it has many parallels with my own. I have been a Christian most of my life and was brought up in a tradition which taught me the value of Bible-reading and study, for which I am very grateful. Discipline comes easily to me and I learned to copy my dad who read his Bible first thing each morning. The evangelical concept of a daily 'Quiet Time' was something which God used to form me and shape me.

I also grew up in the church. So, the communal practices of Bible study and prayer have been a part of my life for as long as I remember – and God has also used them to shave off some of my rough edges and to further shape me.

But it has been in discovering the practices of Renew Wellbeing that I have returned to the simplicity of my relationship with God, both personally and in community. The image of sitting with God with a cup of something warm in my hands, letting him hold me as I hold my day before him, is an image which I find both simple and profound.

And to be able to do that with others, as we each are present to God and to one another, is also both simple and profound. To see others relax in the simplicity of that practice, knowing that nothing is required of them, and then begin to participate in the simple communal practice together, is such a profound experience as we all learn together to simply be – with God and with one another.[12]

It is so lovely and humbling to hear that even for those who have been on the road a while and have good practices in place, the Renew Wellbeing rhythms can bring us back to simplicity in our relationship with God. It is a delight to have Pauline in the Renew family as at the time of writing her Renew space is one of only two in Northern Ireland.

Time to connect
To help us connect in new ways as church, here are a few ideas you may want to use in your communities and groups of church that meet. Here are three ways to engage around this story of Jesus with those you connect with. Being present on your own, being prayerful on retreat and being in partnership with others in a group or gathering.

Be present: To use on your own
Read John 15:1–17 slowly several times. Maybe take a close look at a vine or plant that climbs and clings. Maybe take some fruit and look at it mindfully. See the seeds. Taste the sweetness.

Choose which phrase jumps out at you. As you know for me it is 'fruit that will last' (John 15:16, NIV). Journal around what it is for you and why.

Think about your dwelling or remaining habits. List them.

Maybe choose one I mentioned to engage in, like meditating on psalms, holding a cup as a symbol of being held, practising stillness and silence, using rhythms of prayer or journaling.

Journal or chat or just have a think about the soil you are planted in and the trellis that supports your life. Do you have a Rule of Life? Are there words or phrases or a set of rhythms that might help you be deeply planted in God's love and have fruit that doesn't spoil?

Be prayerful: To use as the basis for a retreat
Take the phrase you have chosen and meditate on it.
Stay, remain, dwell in those words.
Write them down, maybe even draw something that helps you stay with the words or phrase.

If you are using this on retreat alone or with others, you could shape a whole day around some of the various phrases you have highlighted. This is a rich piece of teaching.

Dwell or remain: talk with and listen to God as he chats with you about how to remain. Choose a couple of habits of prayer you might try.

Bear much fruit: go through the fruits of the Spirit in Galatians 5:22–23. Invite the Holy Spirit to fill you with this fruit. Highlight one of the fruits and do some artwork or journaling around this word. Maybe look up the references to the word in Scripture or write your own poem or psalm around this word.

Be in partnership: To use in a group or gathering

If you wanted to use this passage as the basis for a group or whole gathering focus, there are many ways to do it, but in the spirit of the title of this chapter, can I suggest you keep it simple.

Maybe bring in a vine or some grapes.
Do some activities around plants or fruits.
But keep in mind the focus.
Have a key verse or phrase throughout so it doesn't get too complicated.

Maybe have some pieces of actual trellis that people can write on as they explore their own rule of life or rhythms of wellbeing and prayer.

Have a time of prayer and worship using the Psalms and poems you have written, or various songs that talk about dwelling or remaining. Take some time just to listen to some music and soak in God's presence. Make sure there is another option for those uncomfortable with this. Some might like to chat about what they have learned and what they might try.

As a group, maybe decide on a rhythm of prayer and life you could share either together or dispersed. This is what is at the heart of a Renew Wellbeing space.

Take a look at the Renew Wellbeing idea if you aren't familiar with it already, and maybe start planning where and how you could do this to engage fruitfully with your community.

Blessing

May the fruit of your life
Be the fruit that lasts
Quality not quantity
Slow growing, not fast.

May the fruit of your life
Make the finest wine
Not force itself to grow
But just cling to the vine

May the fruit of your life
Produce many seeds
Of peace, joy and love
Of kind and patient deeds

May the taste be
All character
All wellbeing made new
And may your life remain in him
As he remains in you

Vulnerability: Giving Sustainably

To have renewable habits of wellbeing continues to be the experiment of my life. The move away from quick-fix Christianity to a long, slow walk with Jesus includes the fact that my calling to do something about mental and emotional health and the church came when I was at my lowest ebb. We cannot ignore the needs around us, but neither can we try to fix people when we ourselves are often broken. We are all vulnerable because we are all living in a broken world. It took me a long time and a breakdown to realize that I was also human. Sounds ridiculous to say it, really, but I think I felt that as a Christian I should be more than a human, able to overcome every struggle, able to have victory over every worry, able to help anyone, regardless of the impact on myself. I am glad I realized I am vulnerable too. I now own my vulnerability daily and understand myself better, trying to serve and give to others but in ways that are honest, sustainable and more realistic.

So what might it look like to live in a way that makes failure a possibility and weakness an opportunity for God's strength?

I often see lovely Christians put so much pressure on themselves by thinking they have to have wellbeing sorted, so that they can share it from lives that are full of peace and *shalom*. What if we are called because we are a bit broken, to be honest, and to have lifestyles that don't wear us out but show that true wellbeing is a priority of Jesus' followers even on their bad days?

> THOUGHT: The heart of the gospel is forgiveness; therefore it is OK to make mistakes, to be a bit broken and still be called by God.
> QUESTION: How comfortable are you with your own vulnerability?

Connecting with my story: Reflections on over-giving and under-giving in a world of need

To be vulnerable means to be at risk. Many of us have realized the hard way that we are breakable and human. Many of us have also come to understand that this is the very thing we can love, live and lead from.

As we come to look at my favourite of all Jesus' stories, as we come to the call to 'Feed my sheep' that is at the heart of every Christian disciple's activism and overwork, and every Christian leader's passion, I want to invite you to embrace and be honest about your own vulnerability.

Here is a quick reminder of why the charity is called Renew Wellbeing:

> It is . . . genuinely 'OK not to be OK' and still have his renewing going on. It makes sense of the times I have marvelled at the glory shining out of a dying or suffering friend. It gives me great hope that even when I don't care well for myself, he is still renewing me from the inside out. This is what salvation looks like for me. It is a one-off act of love and forgiveness and renewing, but it is also a day-by-day movement of God towards making me new every day, until one day the ultimate renewing will happen . . .
>
> So the whole of creation is precious and not dispensable. It is all being made new. Caring for the planet is vital to our wellbeing too. This is a renewing planet. It matters how we care for it. It matters in itself and it matters to our wellbeing.[1]

My question in this chapter is: what we do about the needs around us that we see, when we are also trying to live well in our own skin as fellow humans and often failing at it? Do we ignore the cry because it overwhelms us? Do we just plough on through our own exhaustion because the needs of others are greater than our own? Is there another way to give and live with wellbeing?

Knowing ourselves to be vulnerable humans is where the concept of renewability is helpful. We are going to need to draw on sources beyond us at times. I have drawn on my own strength, my own love, my own concern and compassion, my own abilities, and they have been finite . . . and I have become exhausted. How do we find ways of living with power sources that are sustainable? Surely this is the power of the Holy Spirit, so how come I broke myself doing what I felt was God's work? If God's power is a renewable source of deep energy and *shalom* for us, why are we so exhausted?

After my recovery, or at least during my recovery when I found myself leaving teaching and beginning to lead the local church full-time, I was constantly at risk of breaking again. I had heard in my own life and the lives of many others the need for a gentler, kinder way of being community, but instead of being gentler and kinder to myself and leading out of those habits, I began a one-woman mission to reinvent every structure that felt difficult for those who were struggling with their mental health. In many ways I am still doing that, but realizing it is not a one-woman mission after all . . . there are loads of us. I have met so many amazing leaders and churches pouring themselves out for the sake of those in need around them. So many of us know that the only renewable source of energy, life and wellbeing is God himself.

But I suppose I am therefore wondering how I got so weary. I am wondering whether more people would be looking for the gentle, beautiful love of Jesus in the church family if we engaged a bit more with what renewable life actually looked like in practice.

For myself, I had been someone who always believed that God renewed me. I had believed since I was a small child that I could come to him at any time, confess sin, be made new. I had preached this gospel, shared this gospel, promoted this gospel, but I wonder if I had really lived this gospel?

Even after I returned to work, and had in place all the rhythms and habits I describe in previous chapters, I still felt the need to serve others, to help and fix others, was in a separate compartment of my life. I would sit alone and practise my meditation, my prayer rhythms, I would take a little time to relax, do a hobby and then head out into my day like an invincible hero ready to stand in the gap for the people.

When I share my story, it can sound like I learned a hard lesson from having a breakdown, and then immediately set up a Renew space to practise what I had learned. In reality, the timing was very much longer.

First, I tried to continue life as I had before, changing nothing except my mindset about mental health. I very soon was back in bed and unwell for a second time.

Then I changed my focus to concentrate more on the most broken, to help those who I knew were struggling the most. This resulted in my ministry becoming an exhausting round of mental health appointments with members of the church, visits to secure units, late-night mercy dashes to sit for hours in accident and emergency waiting rooms with someone in crisis. When I look back, that season of my church-based ministry was spent largely on pastoral care for a few families. I don't regret that. The church were kind and patient enough to let me learn the hard way. The families were, and are, loved by God immensely and are definitely worth the time. It is just that I found it flattering to be the one who could help, and eventually I would also be the one who would let them down. I would be the one who made them think God didn't care enough to keep giving them what they felt they needed. I realized the hard way that if I began over-giving, I had better be ready to keep that up for a lifetime for some of the folk who would be facing a life-time of wellbeing struggles.

I suppose that what I eventually realized was the simple truth that there is a God, and it isn't me! The call to set up a Renew space came from the revelation that I also am human. It came from several years of trying to help people in an unsustainable way. It came as an attempt to be a bit more honest about the power sources I had been tapping into, and the limited supply of energy left in them.

I was drawing on my own experience, my own compassion and my own time. The source of this was still God, but the intention to draw my wellbeing from his *shalom* was a bit weak, to say the least. It was a backdrop to an over-busy life. It was a bass note, not the tune itself. My own contemplative habits were a means to an end, that of helping others, rather than an end in themselves.

My own habits were not translating into shared habits that could see a community of wellbeing emerge with a sustainable and renewable source of wellbeing for all to draw on.

When renew37 began in 2015 I saw the difference shared habits can make. I experienced the relief of renewability in practice, growing from our shared vulnerability, as a community, not just an individual. I also saw that the call to serve others is not a separate thing to the call to live honestly with repentance and an emotional limp.

I had already realized through our small groups and through shared spaces in people's homes that the habits of meditation on Psalms and the rhythms of prayer were something powerful and shareable. It is just that until we set up renew37, I hadn't realized how very core these habits were, and how much more vital they were than so much else we were spending our energy on.

The thing with renewable energy is not simply finding the best source, which for our inner life is God himself by his Spirit. It is also about how we use energy. It is not that the life of God will ever run out, it is that so much of what I was doing was what I would now call 'uncommanded work'. These were things I thought I needed to do, rather than things I was called to. So much activity was also done from false expectations of my own ability. I had experienced healing in slow ways and had a story to share about how to live within God's embrace. But the story was an ongoing one, not a 'beginning, middle, end' one. I had to grasp in those early days that I was still the project. I was not, and never would be, the expert who could go out and pass on that expertise to others. I was a broken vessel that leaked and needed to be constantly renewed myself. I was simply to invite others to join me as I found a way to do this honestly.

Renew spaces became a way for me to live honestly and practise rhythms of wellbeing while also being able to reach out to and be present to those who were in need of help.

It was vulnerability, recognizing my own weakness and lack, and acknowledging my need for God's *shalom*. It was renewability, and it required a change of mind, a change of lifestyle and a change of shared habits.
It still does.

The story I love the most in John's gospel, the one that led me to want to follow this Jesus who cooks breakfast on the beach for his friends, is a story that I find myself reflecting on again around this concept of renewability.

Come with me and spend some time in this story. I know that those who have been on this journey of renewing wellbeing for a while might groan and say that they have heard me wax lyrical about it before! But bear with me. I think this is one of those layered stories that keeps drawing us deeper.

Connecting with his story: When disappointment becomes appointment

Here we find ourselves with the disciples back at their fishing after the resurrection of Jesus. Lots has happened in the previous week, and they must be full of questions as to what it all means. They have returned to what they know, and here we join them.

After this Jesus revealed himself again to the disciples by the Sea of Tiberias, and he revealed himself in this way. Simon Peter, Thomas (called the Twin), Nathanael of Cana in Galilee, the sons of Zebedee, and two others of his disciples were together. Simon Peter said to them, 'I am going fishing.' They said to him, 'We will go with you.' They went out and got into the boat, but that night they caught nothing.

Just as day was breaking, Jesus stood on the shore; yet the disciples did not know that it was Jesus. Jesus said to them, 'Children, do you have any fish?' They answered him, 'No.' He said to them, 'Cast the net on the right side of the boat, and you will find some.' So they cast it, and now they were not able to haul it in, because of the quantity of fish. That disciple whom Jesus loved therefore said to Peter, 'It is the Lord!' When Simon Peter heard that it was the Lord, he put on his outer garment, for he was stripped for work, and threw himself into the sea. The other disciples came in the boat, dragging the net full of fish, for they were not far from the land, but about a hundred yards off.

When they got out on land, they saw a charcoal fire in place, with fish laid out on it, and bread. Jesus said to them, 'Bring some of the fish that you have just caught.' So Simon Peter went aboard and hauled the net ashore, full of large fish, 153 of them. And although there were so many, the net was not torn. Jesus said to them, 'Come and have breakfast.' Now none of the disciples dared ask him, 'Who are you?' They knew it was the Lord. Jesus came and took the bread and gave it to them, and so with the fish. This was now the third time that Jesus was revealed to the disciples after he was raised from the dead.

When they had finished breakfast, Jesus said to Simon Peter, 'Simon, son of John, do you love me more than these?' He said to him, 'Yes, Lord; you know that I love you.' He said to him, 'Feed my lambs.' He said to him a second time, 'Simon, son of John, do you love me?' He said to him, 'Yes, Lord; you know that I love you.' He said to him, 'Tend my sheep.' He said to him the third time, 'Simon, son of John, do you love me?' Peter was grieved because he said to him the third time, 'Do you love me?' and he said to him, 'Lord, you know everything; you know that I love you.' Jesus said to him, 'Feed my sheep.'

John 21:1–17

I love Peter. He is my favourite disciple – if you are allowed favourites. Looking back in the gospels, from the moment he decides to follow Jesus, it is like a competitive sport to him.

Luke 5:1–11 tells us about the first time Jesus got the fish count up for Peter and Peter's response. It is Peter who tells Jesus they haven't caught anything, with what I would imagine to be a bit of an edge in his voice. It is Peter who says they will give it another go because Jesus tells them to. It is Peter who falls to his knees in recognition he is unworthy to be in the presence of the holy. It is to Peter that Jesus says he is changing their career path to fish for people.

Matthew 14:22–33 tells us about the daredevil Peter, who is the one to decide to walk on water in a storm to prove he really believes in Jesus. It is Peter who loses his nerve and sinks. It is Peter who gets wet, but gets saved. It is Peter who sits shivering and bedraggled in the bottom of the boat that as soon as he stepped into it was no longer storm-tossed but bobbing on a calm sea. It is Peter who will be able to say, though, that he actually walked a few steps on water.

Matthew again tells us that it is Peter who first declares who he thinks Jesus is . . . a bold declaration that the others didn't dare to make. It is to Peter that Jesus gives the name 'rock' and the prophecy about his importance to the early church (Matt. 16:16–18).

Mark doesn't tell us a lot about Peter, but does make sure he includes Peter's rebuke from Jesus. It says Peter takes Jesus 'aside' in what I find to be an amusing attempt at power reversal. It is Peter saying that he knows best, Peter trying to rebuke Jesus, even, and correct him.

And for his trouble he gets called 'Satan' by his master (Mark 8:31–33)!

It is Peter who feels the need to break the holy moment on the mountain by suggesting they put up some tents for the divine encounter between Jesus, Moses and Elijah.[2]

It is Peter who feels the need to lash out at Jesus' arrest and cut off an ear. Even though he has spent three years listening closely to the non-violent message of his rabbi.[3]

It is Peter who has said he would never forsake Jesus even if the others did.[4] Peter is one of the two disciples to follow Jesus closely, and he stays nearby after the others have run away following the arrest.[5] And it is Peter who lets Jesus down by denying he even knows him,[6] not once, not twice, but three times.

I feel for him. How often I have tried to be the best disciple I can be, better than I have been before and than others are being, only to find myself being the one who lets him down the most because of my over-offering and headstrong wilfulness.

It is fascinating and hopeful, therefore, that it is to Peter that Jesus makes sure he appears in a fantastic moment of forgiveness and appointment after his resurrection.

I don't just love the fact that Jesus cooks his friends' breakfast, although I really, really love that. I love that this picnic is made by Jesus for his followers. He is the provider, the host, the cook. He has just been to hell and back and he is barbecuing. It is remarkable how Jesus teaches us what it will mean for us to walk well in human skin. There will be beach brunches!

But what I really love is the way Jesus makes this all about Peter. He knows how very disappointed Peter is with himself. He knows that Peter has probably seen himself as a bit of a leader and was probably planning on how he would be able to lead a movement with all the hints he had been given about rocks and church building.

So, Jesus will know that despite having seen him alive before, Peter is counting himself out of the leading game because he has failed. He is planning a return to the old life, picking up the fishing again. Just getting back to safe and normal, if a little cross and disappointed.

Peter has been competing for the title of best disciple ever. And has failed spectacularly. But on hearing it is Jesus on the shore, it is Peter who leaps out of the boat and runs through the sea to Jesus after the miraculous haul of fish, leaving the other disciples to do all the work of bringing in the catch.

It is Peter, when realizing the miraculous catch was actually important, who goes back and drags the whole net ashore (no mean feat), and possibly Peter that counts them and brings some of the catch to share.

This is Jesus showing Peter that the miracles can still happen. That there is no going back. He is inviting Peter to bring what he carries, that his gift is still important, even if he only had something to share after a fish-free night because Jesus made it happen.

Then there is the pause while they eat. No big important conversations happen for a few hunger-filling moments. You can smell the bread on the fire. You can taste the fish. Cold and fed up after a night of fruitless work, amazed and a bit shaken after a miracle they didn't expect, Jesus gives his weary followers a chance to catch their breath and eat their bread. The picnic is not a means to an end, it is Jesus showing that body, mind and soul are linked; that we need to care for ourselves, that our actual hunger as well as our inner soul hunger matters. It is Jesus showing Peter how to integrate the parts of himself he has carefully fragmented and bring the fisher of fish in harmony with the fisher of people. It is a beautiful encounter, and the best bit is yet to come.

Here on the beach in front of the other disciples, who may not even know how badly Peter feels, here in front of the followers who had heard Jesus' rebuke Peter and say he would deny him,[7] here Jesus gently appoints and calls Peter to really follow him and to tend and feed his sheep.[8]

Note that the call to be a sheep-feeder, the call to get involved in serving, in leading, came not at Peter's finest hour but at his lowest moment. He is called in his disappointment to be appointed. It is his failure that kickstarts his real faith adventure.

This I love.

This is a story of new beginnings. This is a story of deep forgiveness. This is a story of Jesus choosing us even though he knows we will fail.

This is vulnerability acknowledged, not hidden.

This is the priority of being someone who knows forgiveness and who knows how to picnic well on undeserved love so that they will be able to feed others.

This is renewability.

This source of life and freedom that Peter finds that day on the beach will not run out for the rest of his natural life because he has understood that he is not being called because he is the best, or because he is gifted, or because he is able . . . he is being called because love is real, the price is paid; there is nowhere he can't come back from.

Peter is realizing that his call to be a rock, to see the church built and to lead others comes out of his inability, vulnerability and failure.

All Jesus needs from him is a declaration of love. Love that is choosing Jesus over the good opinion of others.

Love that is choosing Jesus over the successes of the past. Love that is strong enough to bring him back from the edge of anywhere.

This is why I love Peter. It is not just that his hot-headedness makes me smile and cringe in self-recognition. It is not just that he feels the need to fill the gaps in holy silence with inane camping plans. It is not even the fact that he was the only one brave and stupid enough to walk on water. It is not just his declarations of faith and fidelity. It is the fact that he is chosen *in* the moment of failure and he realizes he is and always will be the project. God has chosen him, even though he really knows him. I can identify with that. A lot!

It is all grace. All miracle. All love.
It is renewable wellbeing offered to every person. It is good news at its best.
We are vulnerable.
We are broken.
We are forgiven.
We are chosen.

We can live with wellbeing and fail badly and be renewed daily . . . and we can serve and teach and feed others without doing violence to our own souls because we are not the source of wellbeing . . . He is.

Our disappointment can become the cultivated ground for his appointment to flourish.

So, anyone can be chosen. Anyone can be appointed. We can all be chosen. We can all be wellbeing-carriers and love-bringers. The source of energy and life supplied will never run out.

If we have bad days, if we fail, if we let him down, then we need to just wait and smell the breakfast cooking. He is coming to forgive, to renew . . . again.

Renewability!

But note in the story that 'Come and have breakfast' comes before 'Feed my sheep'. We are also human. We need to tuck in. We need to recognize that there is a God and it isn't us . . . *before* we start sheep-feeding.

Connecting with our story: Vulnerable church and renewable wellbeing

For all of us who would call ourselves Christian, we are called to be involved in this wonderful renewable wellbeing. In the excellent book *Struggling with God*, addressing why it is vital for churches to prioritize mental and emotional, the authors say:

> Whatever our vocation . . . as a Christian it will be a vocation to pray.[9]

Prayer is something we can all do, and I believe that with prayer at the heart of what we call 'church' we could see amazing things happen. What could a simpler, kinder way of being prayerful church together look like?

I sometimes wonder if it might be possible to shape our gatherings simply on this one story. Imagine with me for a moment a gathering around a fire, around a meal, around something ordinary where we bring what we carry to share, and realize Jesus is the host and that he has already prepared so much.

Imagine food, either real or spiritual or both, being passed round from person to person who bring both their weariness and their gift. Imagine honest conversations about the disappointments and the miracles of the night that has passed.

Imagine this Jesus encounter together with others flowing from our ordinary days and overflowing from our daily practices.

Imagine sharing the Word and letting the truth of it sink in, chatting about its significance, learning from each other.

Imagine giving time to hear the voice of the Lord calling our name, asking us if we love him, bringing us to repentance quietly.

Imagine responding with love in songs and bread and wine and simple prayers of confession and adoration before hearing his call to feed his sheep.

Imagine praying for those not yet with us round the fire, keeping a space for them, choosing to share love with them, to feed and tend each other well. Imagine wrapping some of the fish and bread and taking it to those unable to have been part of the beauty of the meal.

This could be a church I'd like to be part of . . . it could be any church. It might be your church. God is still committed, I believe, to showing his love through his body.

Leaders leading into wellbeing
It has been a privilege to chat with many leaders about wellbeing as a result of my own fascination and journey.

In our recent research, I sent out a survey and asked centres if their leaders were involved in the Renew rhythms fully expecting a lot of negatives, as my sense has been that leaders are running fast and hard and burning themselves out. My researcher bias was on show!

The replies were heartening. Nearly a hundred churches replied which was wonderful, and of those at least a third had regular presence of their minister or full-time leader prioritizing their Renew space. A good proportion of those had the leaders as a key host. I was surprised, but realized I was only asking within the Renew Wellbeing family, so it was more likely that leaders who were seeing the effects of a Renew space would realize its benefits for themselves.

On asking a wider group of leaders, I did find a very broad experience around mental and emotional wellbeing and the effect of leadership on their sense of *shalom*.

I didn't have lots of leaders willing to be interviewed, to be honest, and it may well have been the fact that they thought I had an agenda of selling Renew Wellbeing (fair point . . . although selling would be the wrong word). But I suspect that busyness is another big factor in the lack of availability for comment. Many church leaders are reporting that their stress levels are high and current research[10] bears out the hunch I have that we have returned to an even busier set of practices than before the pandemic. The Barna group reported that in March 2022 42 per cent of pastors had considered leaving ministry in the previous twelve months.[11]

Here are some of the comments from the church leaders who were willing to chat:

> In my training there wasn't any major emphasis on looking after yourself. Mind you, nobody did a module on leading through a pandemic either and we've managed to do that now.

> My top advice as a leader who has struggled with depression would be look after yourself. Love people. Listen well. Give people rest. Get everyone in a small group. Be aware of the need to look after yourself and of the effect of the rubbish life throws at us all.

> I think wellbeing for me is about all the parts of me being at peace with one another.

> I have things that sustain my wellbeing, like my 'how's your heart' peer group that meets monthly.

I think being a leader can help your wellbeing if you are called to it. It can give you a sense of purpose, as long as it doesn't become who you are.

We now have a very strong emphasis on Sabbath. All our team have a Sabbath as well as a day off. Rhythms of life are essential. The pressure to perform often comes from ourselves, not from our churches.

There's a big connect group culture here – 90 per cent of the church are in small groups. In Covid, this was what sustained us. We didn't worry about getting back to Sunday stuff too quickly.[12]

Kathryn's story

The church I lead is set in Leigh Park, Havant, a large council estate of high deprivation (Leigh Park is within the top 5 per cent of the most deprived areas in the UK) where mental wellbeing is often poor. The *shalom* of God's kingdom has been the vision of the church since we arrived in 2014.

I am a wife and mother to two young and beautiful children. My husband has lived with depression for a few years now . . . managing depression, family life and church has been a juggle and a pilgrimage. Mental wellbeing is a high priority for our family and many in the church. The simplicity in the patterns and the opportunity for a safe space are what draws me to Renew.

My awareness of Renew Wellbeing started in January 2021 when 'attending' a Christian leaders' conference. Hearing of Ruth's journey and the simple pattern of a Renew space has been what I personally needed. I could see the benefits and the beauty of being a space to come, be known and to have a safe, quiet space to pray. I felt that night that God said I should be the snail from *The Snail and the Whale!*[13]

Perplexed, I signed up to the book launch of *Slow Down, Show Up & Pray*. That night God had me up between 2 to 3 a.m., with a vision of this being a place of welcome and wellbeing for our community in our dwindling shopping precinct. As a church, we took the opportunity to read the book together and work out if this was something God wanted us to start within our community.

Through 2021 I set it as a priority for my wellbeing for myself to log onto the morning prayer and found it a safe and easy place, a place where I didn't have to lead and could start my working day with a prayer focus. Though life post-Covid doesn't allow for me to log on each day anymore, for me it is a foundation for my day if working at my desk in the morning. We regularly use the morning prayer pattern within the first section of our gathered Sunday worship.

We opened our first Renew space January 2022 within our church building, with the encouragement from Ruth to go slowly, and for it to be a space where it fed me as much as those coming along. I had itchy feet about us being in our building, and continued to look for a home elsewhere. At Easter we moved to a local café (sadly, the café closed in the August; however, we have remained in this community space).

Our space is a simple space; we offer colouring, a puzzle, knitting and crochet each week. Some of our guests are happy to come for the tea and chat. Those who have become firm regulars are those on the edges of our gathered Sunday services. At Renew, it's been wonderful to experience the care hosts give to them, and the support each person offers to others.

Someone who has joined us has often expressed how thankful they are to have found friends who will support them and another, how it is a firm foundation and how they would struggle, being lonely without it. It gives them a place of being safe and wanted.

During 2023 we also started a youth Renew space and this has been really fruitful with the group now trialling a second session due to it being oversubscribed.[14]

Time to connect
To help us connect in new ways as church, here are a few ideas you may want to use in your communities and groups of church that meet. Here are three ways to engage around this story of Jesus with those you connect with. Being present on your own, being prayerful on retreat and being in partnership with others in a group or gathering.

Be present: To use on your own
John 21:1–17 feels like a good story to read outside by
an open fire if possible.
Take time to read the whole story through slowly.
Imagine yourself in the story with the disciples at the
beach breakfast.
Pick out the word or phrase that most strikes you and
meditate on that phrase.

Be prayerful: To use as the basis for a retreat
Take time to dwell in the story and talk to/listen to Jesus
as you sit round (or imagine sitting round!) the campfire.

This could form the basis for a retreat day on your own
or with friends. At the beach, if possible!

Read the passage.
Choose a meditation phrase.
Sit quietly and repeat the phrase.
Hear Jesus asking you to bring some of whatever gift you
carry.
Smell what he has already prepared for you. Name the
gifts he is offering you.
Chat with Jesus about why he also needs what you bring,
if he has already provided so much.
Bring him any sense of failure or any times you feel you
have let him down.
Accept his forgiveness.

Hear him asking if you love him more than 'these'
(John 21:15) . . . what are the 'these' in this sentence for

you? Are there things you love more than him? Talk with him about that.

Hear his call to feed his sheep . . . ask him which sheep. Listen to his heart for his world and what he is asking you to bring to that situation.

Sit quietly with the dying embers of the fire in the presence of Jesus.
Know you are loved and forgiven.

Be in partnership: To use in a gathering or group
To engage with this story with a group or gathering, think about where and how to meet to make it most like a beach picnic or open fire. Of course, this might not be possible in a church building! But you could have food of some sort. This is an ideal one for small groups in homes to gather round a firepit or a barbecue.

- Read or listen to the passage.
- Talk about which parts jumped out at you, which characters you identify with.
- Make sure there are always options for people who don't want to chat: have some simple activities relating to fish, fire, forgiveness, e.g. painting or writing on stones, art with driftwood, beach-related crafts. This can work really well as an all-age time.
- Talk about the fish you are asked to share, to bring . . . about any miraculous provision. Allow space for people to think or share about disappointment too, and try not to answer, just to listen.

- Share thoughts about the breakfast Jesus cooked, and what good things he has prepared for us to sustain our wellbeing.
- Allow some quiet/give space for people to go and chat with Jesus about any disappointments, sin or failure.
- Read some passages about forgiveness, such as Matthew 18:2–22, Luke 15:11–32 or John 8:1–11, and make sure people hear that they are forgiven.
- Maybe consider sharing communion and using some worship songs to tell God how much you love him in the manner that is comfortable for you in your tradition.

Blessing

This breakfast cooked upon the shore
Is just the start
There's more
There's always more

This love feast marks the start of the return
From shattered dreams
Forgiveness
Restoration
Penny-dropping hope
From a life ripped at the seams

Not just a meal to end all meals
Yet starting many more

Not just a glimpse of kindness
Of a Saviour
Who is love right to the core

Not just the blueprint for a lifestyle
That will always feed the poor

But for me
The first meal of a new day
As I take the kingdom keys
He won for me
And open up that door

This feast
These fish
That represent the life I once controlled
Provision I could find and keep and hold
Yes, Lord, I love you more than these

I love you more than fish
That I can find myself
And buy and sell and trade
Accumulating wealth
For me and mine
I love you more
There is no going back
I follow you
I cast my net where you direct
No logic yet no lack

I love you more
I love you most
I love this breakfast that you serve
Sweet Risen Host

To those like me
Who don't deserve

Your daily
Early morning
Everyday
Never-failing
All-forgiving
All-prevailing
Satisfying love

This breakfast that you cook upon the shore
It's just the start
There's more
There's always more

Conclusion: Renewable Wellbeing in Practice

This is for everyone

As I have followed the way of wellbeing that Jesus embodies through these profound stories in John's gospel, I have become even more convinced that the beauty of the good news of God's love for everyone is alive and well. And reading the news today, I also believe this gospel is still what people are hungry to hear and to see lived out in our communities and homes and systems, in our politics and education, in the arts and workplace, in our churches and community spaces. Everyone is hungry for this picnic and we see in our own lives, in the lives of those around us and in the very fabric of our planet, a yearning for a sense of identity, a sigh that there might be a new economy to measure ourselves by, a deep longing for authentic community, a cry of the heart for simplicity and a need not just for renewable energy but for renewable hope and love and purpose, for renewable wellbeing.

It matters little whether people come with a fully formed set of beliefs or just a heart cry to be able to live better as a human with other humans; it seems that when we group together in open spaces that are founded on simple principles and the shared language of wellbeing, then what grows is a seeking after God and life that looks a bit more like the thing Jesus came to start.

We need spaces where everyone can bring and share, where everyone is valued and honoured, where no one is a project to be fixed or a service provider; where there is a recognition of the humanity of every person, then wellbeing can flourish. And everyone can find a place.

In fact, it reminds me so much of the original cry I put down in a poem early on in my own longing for authenticity that I will risk repetition and share that dream with you again:

> I can see a place
> Where all are welcome
> Where family is beyond blood
> Where those who thought they had the least to say
> Least notice taken
> Became most loved
> Most honoured
>
> A place where all seek God
> All seek and find
> His beautiful presence
> And become viral carries
> Infected with his sweet
> Love and grace

A place where we all acknowledge ourselves
As broken
No labels are necessary
Other than human and loved

Where sin is acknowledged
And left behind
And sadness is allowed to be what it is
For as long as it needs to be

Where honesty is the native tongue
And being transcends doing

Where sitting quietly with yourself and God is valued
As much as busying yourself with others

Where the other is seen
Through the eyes of the God
Who made them
And are loved with his compassion

Where simplicity
Gentleness
And joy live
And God is not privatised into meetings

Where we become, all of us
Young and old, co-creators with him

Of small things of beauty
And large systems of justice

Of little works of art
And big works of courage

A place to dream
To imagine
To dare

A place to rest
And pause
And be

A lump of yeast of
Kingdom life
Carrying the DNA of Christ
To every home and workplace

A quiet shared place
Where it's OK not be OK
And where being prayerful, present and in partnership
Breed hope, love and peace.

Where one place
Becomes many places
A web of wellbeing across the nation
I can see a place[1]

The picnic table is spread with good things. Wellbeing is for all.
We need to sit down.

We are also human

It should go without saying, but I feel the need to say it, the church is full of humans! We are not the fourth emergency service, we are a bunch of breakable, flawed humans who love God and want to love him more, who love people and want to love them well. When I say there might be a problem in church, not in Christ, I am aware that it can sound like I am joining the criticism bandwagon of the de-churched, but the writing of this book has brought me to the very humble conclusion that I don't get to have that opinion on someone else's choice of bride. God refers to the church as his 'chosen' people (1 Pet. 2:9), his bride,[2] 'loved by God' (Rom. 1:7), his 'children' (Rom. 8:17–19). I would not take too kindly to someone writing a book criticizing my choice of marriage partner or my kids, believe me . . . I wouldn't buy that book!

God knows what we are like. He knows our shortcomings; he has watched the church be born and toddle and learn and get it horribly wrong. He has watched as his bride staggers off into infidelity and has welcomed her back time and time again. He knows we are human. He made us that way.

I have often said that as a charity we get to be the bridesmaid to the bride. I don't know about you, but I wouldn't say a good bridesmaid points out how awful the bride is looking. They might suggest the brown sack dress was a bad choice; they may offer advice lovingly about the bad decisions they feel are being made. But their role is to support, encourage, strengthen and cheer for the bride, to get her to her bridegroom.

Renew Wellbeing is not church. Our role is like that of a bridesmaid, but we are seeing such beauty it makes it an easier job than we thought.

The church in its many forms is still Christ's bride and the body of Jesus here on the earth. It is time for this body to look after itself a bit better, to speak more kindly of itself, to deal with unhealthy habits and attitudes, to believe its own message and live with the wellbeing that I believe is the very heart of its message.

The picnic is for us too. We need to be partakers if others are to know that it is as good as we say it is.

We need to tuck in.

The good news is the gospel of wellbeing
The biggest reason that I would love everyone to join the picnic, to prioritize wellbeing personally and corporately, to model and offer spaces of wellbeing in their communities is that I believe it is the very heart of what Jesus came to bring us, teaches us to embody and to win for us – abundant life.[3]

Looking at these stories of Jesus in John's gospel, I have been able to see parallels with the results of the research done by the New Economics Foundation in 2008 and the continued language used by mental health services.

The Five Ways to Wellbeing that we began the book with are seen in these simple picnic stories of Jesus. I don't want to reduce the beauty of these amazing God encounters to just five simple phrases or words, but because I believe this is a message for everyone and that we are also human, I want to make sure I keep grounding the truth of the gospel in everyday reality.

Identity: The story of Jesus changing water into wine and the lessons learned about the identity of this God made flesh and his desire to respond to our need and be part of our everyday lives in a story of **connection**. To connect with this God in our lives, we will also need to connect with ourselves and those around us.

Economy: The story of Jesus meeting that woman at the well in Samaria is a story of keeping on **learning**. We need to learn from this Jesus how to sit down when we are weary, how to ask for help, how to honour the other. We need to learn from this woman how to be brave enough to stay in the encounter, to risk trusting again, to be accepted as we are. We need to learn constantly from the other, the value of one, the economy of small and the success criteria of the way of the cross.

Community: This story of 5,000 being fed by so little is a story of **getting active**, but getting active with what we have, not what we don't have. It points to the need to hand over what we carry to God, not to try to fix things ourselves. It points to the need we all have for the gift of each other and how we don't always need to be the one carrying the picnic.

Simplicity: This teaching Jesus shares with his followers before he goes to the cross about fruitfulness is calling us into simpler ways of clinging to the source of life and away from programmes and busyness. The fruit of our lives can become tasteless when we try to grow it ourselves; the dwelling, the remaining takes some habits that we can stick to and share. This off-stage life, the roots of who we are need to be in his deep love. This is **taking notice** daily, hourly and bringing ourselves back to basics.

Vulnerability: This wonderful breakfast on the beach forgiveness story of a broken, disappointed man being appointed to lead a movement draws us all into the possibility of renewed wellbeing and purposeful **giving**. We cannot give what we haven't received, and we cannot give if we don't hear the call of the Giver in even our most broken moments reminding us there is a God and it isn't us.

Shalom is not a feeling but a fact of the gospel and the very character of God. We can dwell in it and it can dwell in us, not because we do all the habits in the book but because he loves us and chooses us and pursues us and woos us.

All wellbeing can be renewed. The cross was not the end. Jesus faced what had to be faced for us knowing that the 'It is finished' (John 19:30) could put an end to fear and shame and guilt and death for all of us forever. We may still have to go the way of the cross; life is still a breakable thing for now, but we need not fear because resurrection is the last word. Wellbeing, peace, *shalom* is renewable because of that amazing work of beating death and shame and fear that Jesus did that day.

The word *shalom* in the Hebrew that I think is the best way to explain what we are searching for when we talk about wellbeing, is from the root that also means 'paid in full'. This is the good news that these simple principles lead me back to. This is the *shalom* that is possible for everyone. This is what we are seeing lived out in our Renew centres.

It doesn't yet look like an end to all suffering and pain and tears, but it will one day. And because of that we can rant, we can cry, we can be honest and we are still held in a love that will never fail, never let us go.

In the words of God, whispered in my ear all those years ago: 'I couldn't love you any more and I will never love you any less' – spoken to me in my broken empty year of burnout, when I was doing *nothing*.

This is a table laid before us in the presence of the enemy that is despair, depression and low mood. This is a feast for the soul on dark days and lonely moments, when the enemy tells us we are beaten.

> The Lord is my shepherd; I shall not want.
> He makes me lie down in green pastures.

He leads me beside still waters
He restores my soul.
He leads me in paths of righteousness,
for his name's sake.

Even though I walk through the valley of the shadow of death
I will fear no evil,
for you are with me;
your rod and your staff,
they comfort me.

You prepare a table before me
in the presence of my enemies;
you anoint my head with oil;
my cup overflows.
Surely goodness and mercy shall follow me
all the days of my life,
and I shall dwell in the house of the LORD
for ever.

Ps. 23

This is good news. There is nothing at all wrong with the gospel.

The *shalom* he offers us is renewable. The source will never ever run out.

The picnic is possible, it is prepared for us, we are invited to join in. God is already doing this thing. It's not really our picnic site. It is his.

We need to feed . . . ourselves and others.

There is enough. There will always be enough.

The Renew Wellbeing story

Don't just take my word for it. Here are some of the comments from around the UK when I asked in our recent survey: 'What has been good about your Renew space?'

> We have seen lives changed. We have seen people come to faith, and because we partner with more than mental health teams, one story which comes to the mind is of someone who suffered with such anxiety that they were sweating and shaking when they first came. Their partner had been unable to work for a long time because they couldn't leave this person on their own. As they become more and more confident, the partner was supported by our employment support team member, who helped them back into employment. The person now comes to café either with a friend or even sometimes alone. Our craft table has been very significant for them as they are very creative and it has been their safe space.

> We are seeing non-church people come in from our local community, grow in confidence, find their voice, find friends and somewhere to belong – a safe space.

> I love the way guests have made friends and support each other, it's a safe space which everyone enjoys attending. It doesn't feel like work, it feels as if we provide the space and the people come! I love the way that people who say they don't have a faith come into the prayer space and appreciate it.

> What do I love about Renew? God showing up. His presence is tangible and we have seen people responding to him in different ways; some people have found a degree

of healing; one said that Renew has been their lifeline. There is a real sense of family there.

It is supporting my own mental wellbeing as well as those who come each week. I love the fact that new people are welcomed and 'absorbed' organically into the group and that deep friendships are being formed, where people look out for each other. Our final prayer time is where I pray for each person by name – last week we had twenty-four people at Renew, eighteen of whom came to prayers because they want to hear their name as I pray for them. I need a prompt to remember everyone as they are quick to check I've mentioned each person! I love that!

Hard to pick one thing, so here are some!
Volunteers who understand what Renew is about and do it so well.
Seeing folk:

- becoming more connected with others
- helping each other
- trying new activities
- becoming volunteers

and hearing them time and time again comment on the welcoming, calm and friendly atmosphere. Guess the best thing is that despite some challenging weeks (which probably will continue!), all the hosts agree that we can see God's faithfulness to Renew every week.

Bringing people into the church building and to some events, including Sundays, who would never have stepped inside in a million years normally. They now consider the group to be their own, and regulars are bringing others in the community for help. Being able to offer support via the parish nurse and other organizations in our area.

Getting to know people. Helping others who need a bit of extra support. Just having the door open so that anyone can come into a quiet space and experience God's love in action, even if they don't know him. Seeing lives transformed. Being still and focusing on God in our quiet prayer times.

It is as much a space for the hosts as it is for the regulars. We can all attend to our wellbeing and value the time away from our 'day job'.

Being able to sit with our regulars and chat.
We run a coffee morning on Tuesdays and that is really busy, noisy, joyous, etc. We are happy to serve, but don't get much time to chat.
In our Renew space we are all together and we can chat as we colour, etc.
We have a number of support workers who come in with their clients – it is lovely to see them relax for a short time.
I *love* the prayer times.

The people who have come feeling helpless and find hope, then become part of the team and want to give back what they have received.[4]

The final word goes to those who are joining the picnic and finding life, those who might not have found Christ in the box we have put him in and called it 'church', but have found him as we began to slow down, show up and pray in simpler ways. These quotes and stories come from just two of our wonderful centres. There are many more stories out there, too.

I never thought it would be my thing, but I've loved it, so welcoming. And so, here I am.

When I go out from my time here, I genuinely feel my mood uplifted.

. . . and I told him, you will have to go. It's Renew and I'm not missing that for anything. Come with me if you want.

Quiet space is so very peaceful; I could just sit in there for hours. No pressure, just calm.

We've had one guest who, when they first arrived was at a very low place in life and on the verge of suicide. They had never known faith, but for some reason felt they should come . . . they became a regular at our Renew space and began to ask questions like, 'Why is Jesus so important at the Baptist church?' They formed a close friendship with one of our other guests who was struggling . . . Over the next few weeks and months God turned this person's life around miraculously – they came to faith, found work, found new hope and purpose in life and is about to be baptized!

Another guest has multiple struggles in life and Renew is one of the few places they feel able to come out to regularly. We've shared with them the ups and downs of life – including just recently the birth of a grandchild. One day, at the end of our prayer time (where we use a very simple prayer rhythm from Psalm 103), they said, 'This place is like a big warm blanket.' Another week, as we sat quietly at the end of our prayers, they breathed deeply and said, 'I don't want to leave.' To know that Renew gives people a space where they feel safe and at home, and can experience the peace of God in our prayers, is such an encouragement.[5]

My prayer as Renew centres multiply is that God renews our wellbeing so much that the church is at the heart of every community's *shalom*. As I write these words, I am sitting in a lovely shepherd's hut near Holy Island where I have spent a day on retreat. As I arrived on the island, I was drawn away from the crowds arriving to sit on my own on the beach. To be honest, I was irritated by how many people were there. I wanted some alone time. But after chatting with God, I realized this was the very thing he wanted to talk to me about. This is the point of this book, really. We are not islands. We need each other. God loves his church. He is renewing us. He still believes in us.

God's wellbeing connects us, teaches us, gets us active, helps us take notice and ultimately involves giving. Reading about Aidan and Cuthbert and other pioneering saints who established worshipping communities before us, I am understanding that this renewability, this need to know our identity, measure with new economy, live with simplicity and vulnerability will require us to be part of community. But what that community looks like may well need to change so that those who feel excluded can belong, so that the next generation can embrace the beauty of shared life, so that all may see and know the One who called us together as the community of wellbeing, so that those who are so alone, so forgotten, might be most honoured and find home.

I spent time in three very different places on the island. Firstly, I found a bench where twos and threes could chat without prearrangement. Then I found a coffee roastery and café where groups could meet informally at any time. Finally, I sat and prayed in St Mary's church, where gatherings happened across the day.

I realize that as well as personally responding to the need for wellbeing in my life to be a priority, I need all three types of space to connect with others. The small and unplanned get-togethers, sometimes with complete strangers, allow me to grasp the moment to share a bit of journey and learn from another. The more relaxed spaces allow us to connect and enjoy real life together, and pray across many different sorts of people. The church building or gathering space enables shared expression of worship and learning to happen. All three of these types of space bless God and strengthen us. All three are needed, I think, and it needs to be clearer for all how they can access and be welcomed into these sorts of spaces to engage in shared wellbeing. The picnic is for everyone.

There are bigger conversations going on about what gatherings might look like that could grow out of these simple Renew spaces. For a full transcript of a recent chat between two of our team members who are experimenting with Renew-shaped church, please have a look in Appendix Four.[6]

As a Baptist leader recently said, 'Do set up Renew Wellbeing spaces but be prepared for them to change the whole way you do church . . . in a good way.'

Wellbeing is not a snack. It is the whole picnic.

Knowing who we are and who he is, measuring with his values, not ours, being together, not isolated, adopting simple habits, and knowing forgiveness means that failure is most definitely an option, all adds up to renewable wellbeing. These big issues, if addressed honestly and consistently in our churches, might just give us a way to wellbeing that everyone in our communities could get hungry for. This amazing gospel of wellbeing is spread out like a picnic, as simple as a picnic, as shareable as a picnic.

These simple shifts in culture will not be easy in an overbusy, success-driven world, but I believe these are the shifts I am beginning to see in the Renew Wellbeing movement, and it fills me with hope. God loves his church. He loves his world. He is fully committed to making 'all things new' (Rev. 21:5).

This is renewable wellbeing.

Renewability: A Blessing

May you know who you are
Fix your gaze on his face

May you measure your worth
With the plumbline of grace

May you find real community
Not journey alone

May your habits be simple
May your life be God's home

May wellbeing surround you
And fill you each day

May you know you are called
May he teach you to pray

And remember the picnic
Is also for you
Sit down, tuck in, feed
For you're human too.

Appendix One

Poems from the Renew Wellbeing Family[1]

Susanna's poem

Susanna is a facilitator for Renew Wellbeing employed by a Baptist association to work with us to promote the idea of Renew spaces. She wrote this great poem in response to reflections on us as God's dwelling place.

Dwell: The Church

In all its messiness, dysfunction and hurt
Even there, God dwells.
Gathered together, that extra dimension
He speaks, he heals, he touches.
Gathered locally *and* in the church worldwide
The churches I strongly disagree with
Those where I feel at home
Whatever the denomination, whoever the leader
Whether led well or fallen from grace
Here he dwells!
Lord, show us your presence.

Susanna Hinton, 2023

Sarah's poem

Sarah joins us daily to pray, even though at the time of writing she does not have a Renew centre to attend. She is learning first the simple rhythms of prayer. Sarah is blind and here writes a poem about how her other senses bring her deeply into God's presence. It is a beautiful poem. We are grateful to Sarah for all she is teaching us and hopefully by the time you are all reading this, she will have a Renew space to play and pray in too.

Headphones wrapping around my ears,
we begin the day with a psalm,
blessing God with our very selves.

Blips on a screen unite to pray;
in just a word or a sentence,
complex thoughts are simply expressed.

Scent of coffee from my machine,
I take a sip; savour its strength –
my hands cradling the warm mug.

We lift our eyes from the mundane
to see God as our Redeemer,
naming places that need his touch.

We bask in the glorious truth
God crowns us with love, compassion –
feel the weighty crown on my head.

Sarah Tummey, June 2023

Adrienne's poem

Adrienne hosts a lovely Renew space in Wales. Here is her heartfelt expression of why prayer is so vital for her wellbeing.

I need words
Not to impress
But to confess
'Holy is he'

I cast about
Amid your glorious beams
For one to pierce
My weary ragged heart

Achieving nothing
I slow down, cool down, breathe
Await your tapping
Swishing through my soul
To seal and know again
That you are
Real

Other mornings
As I wake
You are
Already there.
Holy O holy
'Holy is he'

Adrienne, June 2023

Appendix Two

Setting Up Renew Spaces and Multiplication

Hosts and Area Coordinators
Renew Wellbeing spaces are led by hosts trained using resources from www.renewwellbeing.org.uk.

The manual for setting up centres is available in the book *Slow Down, Show Up & Pray* by Ruth Rice. These centres are supervised by their local church and networked with other centres locally by the area coordinator from the Renew Wellbeing team for encouragement and review. Contact mandy@renewwellbeing.org.uk for further information.[1]

Local Links
Role description for a Renew Wellbeing Local Link:

A Local Link is a voluntary role for a Christian who attends a local church and is part of a Renew project, or has completed the training and understands what a Renew centre is, and wants to help encourage churches locally to get started with Renew and maintain simple, safe, sustainable practices.

The 5, 4, 3, 2, 1 of local linking:

> **5** supporting up to five churches/projects to include the Local Link's home project;
> **4** four meetings a year (quarterly) with other Local Links and Renew team;
> **3** three principles to encourage/support (presence, prayer, partnership);
> **2** two hours a month should be enough to fulfil the role
> **1** '*one thing* is needed' (Luke 10:41–42, NKJV, emphasis mine). Committed to habits of wellbeing/prayer.

An area coordinator will spot a Local Link as someone who is keen to help support the work of the charity, and the area coordinator will invite the person to a Zoom meeting to explain the role and set up a support process for them (e.g. one phone call a month, a meeting with other Local Links once a quarter).

It is hoped that the Local Links will work with the area co-ordinator to see strong local connections and networks develop that help Renew spaces keep going for a long time, and multiply.

Hubs
What is a Renew Wellbeing hub?

A Renew hub church is a resourcing church with its own experience of running a Renew space for at least a year.

A Renew hub church has the capacity to receive interested visitors once a month to see their Renew space (after hours).

A Renew hub church is a centre for support, encouragement and prayer locally for a network of Renew spaces.

Each Renew hub church:

- has recognized good practice in their own Renew centre
- has some capacity to receive visiting teams (monthly after sessions)
- has a named leader who is coached by the charity director/area coordinator
- has a Wellbeing Local Link associated with the hub willing to travel locally to do visits and reviews (the hub leader can also be the Local Link if they have time)
- has the willingness to host a get-together of the network monthly on Zoom or in-person

Facilitators
Role purpose:

- to establish a Renew Wellbeing presence across a certain organization's churches and missional communities
- to identify churches and key partners in Renew Wellbeing as a way of churches engaging with their communities
- employed by the organization concerned with an agreed partnership with Renew Wellbeing.

Appendix Three

Resources for Children, Youth and Family Renew

A few years ago, we were beginning to be asked the question, 'Can we do Renew with young people?' Under-18s are struggling more than ever with mental and emotional wellbeing and we wanted to offer our help.

To investigate whether Renew for Children, Young People and their Families (CYF) could be established, Sarah from the Renew team began some groundwork, including lots of research, trials and working with others using different models and practices. Careful consideration was needed to ensure it could be done in a safe way for our guests and Renew spaces, as well as working within the Renew ethos of being present, prayerful and in partnership. We also felt this would be great for churches that have already completed the Renew training for adults, and have opened a space to further expand on what they can offer in their community.

We were thrilled to be able to launch our CYF model at our June 2021 Renew Family Gathering. If you think this may be something your church could offer, or if you would like more information, please *register your interest with us.*

We have a training package available in the form of a manual, followed by three further training videos specific for working with under-18s.[1]

Appendix Four

Renew-shaped Church? A Conversation

This is a full transcript of one of the conversations be-
tween two area coordinators who also lead churches,
Margaret and Mary, who are experimenting with
Renew-shaped gatherings on Sundays as well as a Renew
Wellbeing space in the week.[1]

Transcript
**Q: What might church look like if it grew from our
Renew spaces?**

Margaret
So, a group of us have been chatting about that question.
What if church could look and feel more like our Renew
spaces? The group kind of came about because various
things were already happening within churches. Maybe
for some churches they were looking at their people in
their Renew space who might like or benefit from coming
to some kind of church gathering but wouldn't find tra-
ditional church or anything that looks like that very easy
to access. So, some groups have sort of experimented

with forms of worship outside of their worship space; for others of us, it's been a case of: 'How do we let this culture of Renew impact all of life as church?' really, but including our worship spaces on Sunday, and we've been reflecting a little bit like around that.

Q: So, Mary, do you want to share a little bit about what's been happening where you are?

Mary
We've started a once-a-month Renew-type service which is a bit more relaxed. We have the activities out, there's always colouring, and we just go through one of the letters from the *A–Z of Wellbeing*. So we summarise the chapter. We'd look at the Word of God. We'd look at how it could relate and, if the people are comfortable, there are one or two questions they can discuss on their table. They do that, we feed back. Sometimes I would pick up the main points, summarize and then we would just listen to a reflective song and let God speak to people individually, just quietly in that space. And then we go back to having tea, coffee sometimes. It's quite relaxed; that's the idea, that people would feel comfortable coming in . . .

Margaret
Brilliant. I think ours has kind of come about a little bit more accidentally than that, almost . . . because I found myself for a season taking the leadership of a network of small churches, with one particularly active church in

the centre of all of that, where we have a morning service and we've had some young families come and join us – there's not many of us. I'm talking about probably around twenty people. But we have really needed simplicity, because a lot of our people are just burned out, so we've needed to look at some more sustainable ways of doing and being church that creates a welcome for people, that enables people of all ages and backgrounds to share together and to be family . . . Our Renew thinking has certainly been feeding into that . . . It's not about a sort of set way of doing Renew church. It's about allowing that thinking from our Renew spaces to infiltrate what we do in our main service, and that's likely to be different for every context. Mary, yours is different to ours and it's a work in progress.

Q: What would you feel are the biggest challenges with yours at the moment?

Mary
I think getting people from our Renew space to our Sundays, but part of our church are benefiting as well from that slightly more relaxed style, although most of our services are relaxed nowadays. But that gentler, softer approach where they can just come and sit and be is great. But really, I'd like more people to discover that sitting and being in family with God.

Margaret
Cool. Yeah, we've got the people coming. We have . . . these families come and join us. We've also got a little

coffee space down the corridor . . . one of our new regulars has been popping in and sitting drinking coffee in that space, not actually joining us, although they can hear everything that's going on. But just having a space down the corridor to feel safe – and then somebody else within our service who actually sometimes needs to go out and just feel safe in their own space, and they go and join them. And that's been a really lovely thing, but I don't know how that developed. I think our biggest challenge has been that we've so quickly got back into those habits of busyness. We think, 'OK, we've got these families, we need to do all these amazing activities and all these whizzy things, and we need to spend lots of time preparing.' And sometimes there'd be crazy WhatsApps going on a Saturday, trying to prepare for Sunday. So we're still working out how we find content, but with that wonderful welcome for everybody. We've got ideas. We're trying different things. We're looking at different resources because there's quite a lot out there. We've gone into having two zones now. So for a lot of the service we're together, but then we have a quiet zone where there's a more traditional-type sermon. I'd love to see that move on to a shorter sermon with a bit more time for chatting together and a family zone where the children and their parents are learning together, really, and having a lot of fun . . . The other week we were playing with gloop and making a right mess, thankfully in the back garden. It was for a purpose, of course!

Q: What do you hope for the future, for your space – in your Renew space and how you might worship coming out of that?

Mary

Gentleness, I think, is one word I do feel God is sort of speaking. People just feel that. Accessibility. The ability to come and not be forced into anything, and not be frightened that they don't know what to do, because it's church and you have to do things. But people can just come and be and enjoy being part of our family because we do [that] within our group of people who come regularly. We have a really good family feel and we'd like the family to get bigger.

Margaret

I think I share that and I'd love to see us grow. We have got this exciting growth going on among our young families. I'd like to see more cohesiveness between our ages, and that's something we're working on developing, and simplicity. Truly finding simple ways . . . to make people welcome, and I think possibly services that are a little shorter; we're trying to share the load a lot more. So, trying to identify giftings across what isn't a very big community. We've got somebody making playdough this week. But that does take forward planning. So yes, the forever looking for simplicity and forever questioning ourselves on, have we lost that? And if so, how can we find it again? So, I think that's where we're at, but it is an ongoing conversation, and if this has struck a chord with anyone listening, if there's something like this happening in your context, then do get in touch through the website, www.renewwellbeing.org.uk, and you're very welcome to join our conversation, which happens around every three or four months or so. So, it's been good to chat. Mary, thank you.

Join this conversation online by contacting Renew Wellbeing through the website contact page, www.renewwellbeing.org.uk

Bibliography

Aked, Jody, Nic Marks, Corrina Cordon, Sam Thompson. *Five Ways to Wellbeing*, New Economics Foundation, 22 October 2008. https://neweconomics.org/2008/10/five-ways-to-wellbeing (accessed 5 August 2021).

Bonhoeffer, Dietrich. *Life Together* (London: SCM Press, 1954).

Boyd, Greg. *Present Perfect* (Grand Rapids, MI: Zondervan, 2010).

Brown Taylor, Barbara. *An Altar in the World* (Norwich: Canterbury Press, 2017).

Brown Taylor, Barbara. *Leaving Church* (London: Canterbury Press, 2011).

Brueggemann, Walter. *The Prophetic Imagination* (Minneapolis, MN: Augsburg Fortress, 2001).

Cook, Christopher, Isabelle Hamley, John Swinton. *Struggling with God* (London: SPCK, 2023).

Cook, Christopher, Isabelle Hamley (eds). *The Bible and Mental Health* (London: SCM Press, 2020).

Greig, Pete. *How to Pray* (London: Hodder & Stoughton, 2019).

Jelley, Nick. *Renewable Energy* (Oxford: Oxford University Press, 2020).

Lawrence, Brother and Frank Laubach. *Practicing His Presence* (Jacksonville, FL: SeedSowers, 1973).

Nouwen, Henri. *The Way of the Heart* (New York: HarperOne, 1981).

Nouwen, Henri. *In the Name of Jesus* (London: Darton, Longman & Todd, 1989).

Rice, Ruth. *Slow Down, Show Up & Pray* (Milton Keynes: Authentic, 2021).

Rice, Ruth. *A–Z of Wellbeing* (Milton Keynes: Authentic, 2022).

Roberts, Richard. *Cultivating God's Presence* (Dorset: Finnian Press, 2021).

Rupp, Joyce. *The Cup of Our Life* (Notre Dame, IN: Ave Maria Press, 1997).

Swinton, John. *Spirituality and Mental Health Care* (London: Jessica Kingsley Publishers, 2001).

Willard, Dallas. *Renovation of the Heart* (Nottingham: IVP, 2002).

End Notes

Introduction

[1] Ruth Rice, *Slow Down, Show Up & Pray* (Milton Keynes: Authentic, 2021).

[2] Ruth Rice, *A–Z of Wellbeing* (Milton Keynes: Authentic, 2022).

[3] www.renewwellbeing.org.uk (accessed 6 November 2023).

[4] https://www.nationalchurchestrust.org/news/holy-spirit-uk-has-more-churches-pubs (accessed 1 November 2023).

[5] Brother Lawrence, *The Practice of the Presence of God* (Eastford, CT: Martino Fine Books, 2016).

[6] 'OK not to be OK' – origin of this phrase not confirmed, but thought to be first used commercially in 2011 by Hope for the Day, www.hftd.org (accessed 29 May 2020).

[7] Renew Wellbeing is a national charity that helps churches set up spaces of belonging for all, particularly those with mental health challenges. www.renewwellbeing.org.uk (accessed 6 November 2023).

[8] *Shalom*, https://biblescan.com/search.php?q=shalom (accessed 25 May 2023).

[9] renew37 is a church run space in West Bridgford, Nottingham, staffed and funded by New Life Baptist Church www.renew37.co.uk (accessed 6 November 2023).

[10] renewwellbeing.org.uk registered charity number 1173963. In Scotland, OSCR SC049975.

[11] Five Ways to Wellbeing. New Economics Foundation and the government's Foresight project, http://neweconomics.org/2008/10/five-ways-to-wellbeing-the-evidence/ (accessed 8 July 2021). Permission given to use Five Ways to Wellbeing with thanks to New Economics Foundation and the government's Foresight project, 15 July 2021.

[12] See Luke 10:6.
[13] Edited for the purposes of this book.

Chapter One
[1] https://www.simplypsychology.org/erik-erikson.html (accessed 1 November 2023).
[2] See Rice, *Slow Down, Show Up & Pray* and *The A–Z of Wellbeing*.
[3] 'Fuzzy Felt' was a children's activity with characters and backdrop to retell stories with sticky felt.
[4] See John 14:6.
[5] John 1:41,45.
[6] John 1:23–27.
[7] Brother Lawrence, *The Practice of the Presence of God*.
[8] Edited for the purposes of this book.
[9] Renew Wellbeing.
[10] Christian retreat centre. See https://ffald-y-brenin.org/ (accessed 1 November 2023).
[11] See Matt. 11:28–30, MSG.
[12] Edited for the purposes of this book.
[13] www.retreats.org.uk (accessed 1 June 2023).
[14] Renew Wellbeing Daily prayers available free on www.renew-wellbeing.org.uk (accessed 6 November 2023).
[15] Rice, *A–Z of Wellbeing*, pp. 141–51.
[16] renewwellbeing.org.uk/get-involved (accessed 1 June 2023).

Chapter Two
[1] Rice, *Slow Down, Show Up & Pray*, p. 18.
[2] Rice, *A–Z of Wellbeing*, pp. 163–65.
[3] Rice, *A–Z of Wellbeing*, p. 164.
[4] See 1 Cor. 12 and 14 where spiritual gifts are discussed. Prophetic words and pictures are often a manifestation of something God wants to show his people, individually or corporately.
[5] Edited for the purposes of this book.
[6] A Local Link is a volunteer who wants to help other churches sustain their Renew spaces and to promote Renew Wellbeing in their area. See Appendix Two.

[7] Baptist Union of Great Britain.

[8] Social Prescribing is described by the NHS as a way to connect services with people who need to use them. Social prescribers are hired to make these connections. See www.england.nhs.uk/personalisedcare (accessed 10 November 2023).

[9] See Ps. 90:17.

[10] Edited for the purposes of this book.

[11] Edited for the purposes of this book.

[12] Edited for the purposes of this book.

Chapter Three

[1] Mike Royal, 'How to Halt the Decline', 26 April 2022, https://www.premierchristianity.com/features/how-to-halt-the-decline/12937.article (accessed 1 November 2023).

[2] Jordan Kelly-Linden, 'People are Increasingly Turning to Religion to Find Meaning, Research Shows', 22 May 2020, https://www.telegraph.co.uk/global-health/climate-and-people/pandemic-prompts-surge-interest-prayer-google-data-show/ (accessed July 2023).

[3] Read about this more in Rice, *Slow Down, Show Up & Pray*, pp. 26–44.

[4] Matt. 18:20.

[5] https://www.bbc.co.uk/programmes/b0bhkc8b (accessed 2 November 2023).

[6] 1 Cor. 14:26.

[7] https://www.campaigntoendloneliness.org/facts-and-statistics/ (accessed 2 November 2023).

[8] https://www.bps.org.uk/psychologist/psychology-friends (accessed 2 November 2023).

[9] https://www.mentalhealth.org.uk/explore-mental-health/statistics/relationships-community-statistics (accessed 2 November 2023).

[10] 1 Cor. 12:27.

[11] Rice, *Slow Down, Show Up & Pray*, p. 148.

[12] https://www.eauk.org/news-and-views/mission/page/2 (accessed 9 June 2023).

[13] https://www.quora.com/How-many-Christian-churches-are-there-in-the-world (accessed 2 November 2023).

[14] Some names have been changed to protect identities.
[15] Edited for the purposes of this book.
[16] Edited for the purposes of this book.
[17] Renew Wellbeing Survey June 2023 conducted by Ruth Rice using Mailchimp survey.
[18] Edited for the purposes of this book.

Chapter Four

[1] Rice, *A–Z of Wellbeing*, pp. 79–87.
[2] Matt. 3:8; Luke 3:8; John 15:16.
[3] https://biblehub.com/greek/3306.htm (accessed 15 June 2023).
[4] John 10:10.
[5] https://www.northumbriacommunity.org/who-we-are/our-rule-of-life/what-is-a-rule-of-life/ (accessed 2 November 2023).
[6] A person trained in spiritual companionship.
[7] Ffald-y-Brenin, *Rhythm of Daily Prayer* (Pembrokeshire: Ffald-y-Brenin Media, 2015).
[8] A prayer to reflect on the events of the day, with God.
[9] Barbara Brown Taylor, *Leaving Church* (London: Canterbury Press, 2011), p. 111.
[10] Edited for the purposes of this book.
[11] Edited for the purposes of this book.
[12] Edited for the purposes of this book.

Chapter Five

[1] Rice, *A–Z of Wellbeing*, p. 201.
[2] Mark 9:5.
[3] John 18:10.
[4] Matt. 26:33–35.
[5] John 18:15.
[6] John 18:15–27.
[7] Matt. 26:33–35.
[8] John 21:15–17.
[9] Christopher Cook, Isabelle Hamley, John Swinton, *Struggling with God* (London: SPCK, 2023), p. 5.
[10] https://www.churchtimes.co.uk/articles/2023/13-january/news/uk/clergy-well-being-falling-study-shows (accessed 3 November 2023).

11 https://www.barna.com/research/pastors-quitting-ministry/ (accessed 3 November 2023).

12 Edited for the purposes of this book.

13 Julia Donaldson, *The Snail and the Whale* (London: Puffin Books, 2006).

14 Edited for the purposes of this book.

Conclusion

1 Rice, *Slow Down, Show Up & Pray*, pp. 147–49.

2 Eph. 5:25–27.

3 John 10:10.

4 Edited for the purposes of this book.

5 Edited for the purposes of this book.

6 Margaret and Mary are both area coordinators who have also led churches. Renew Wellbeing spaces will never be church. They need to stay as spaces that are any faith and none with a prayer space. But gatherings that use the Renew model are emerging as people come to faith through Renew spaces.

Appendix One

1 Poems edited for the purposes of this book.

Appendix Two

1 Information in this appendix has been taken from our website, https://www.renewwellbeing.org.uk (accessed 14 November 2023). Edited for the purposes of this book.

Appendix Three

1 https://www.renewwellbeing.org.uk/cyf (accessed 14 November 2023). Renew Children Youth and family training has been written by Sarah Fegredo, who is part of the Renew Wellbeing national team.

Appendix Four

1 Edited for the purposes of this book.

Authentic

We trust you enjoyed reading this book from Authentic. If you want to be informed of any new titles from this author and other releases you can sign up to the Authentic newsletter by scanning below:

Online:
authenticmedia.co.uk

Follow us:

Milton Keynes UK
Ingram Content Group UK Ltd.
UKHW031544071024
449381UK00014B/191

9 781788 933568